C000016532

M. L

GENEALOGY COLLECTION

PECULIAR INHERITANCE

A History of the Elmhirsts

1951

FOREWORD

THE dale of Worsbrough, lying south of the bleak black city of Barnsley in the West Riding of Yorkshire, is the scene on which this history was enacted. To-day the land is treeless, coal trucks move far underground, opencast mining gnaws the surface and vomits back the earth, noise and dirty smuts gloom the air on an evil wind.

Continuity seems out of place in such surroundings. Feudal lords and greedy Church long ago lost their holdings there to an all-powerful throne and its progeny of new-made squires; the industrial revolution supplanted these with its own grim spawn of ironmasters and traders grown rich with coal; now these in turn have loosed their grasp to drab anxious men who live in Worsbrough Hall and manage for the Welfare State. But in this valley the family of Elmhirst, one of the very few that has uninterruptedly held the place from which it got its name, alone is left alive to flourish and protect the land.

My indebtedness to many will be apparent to anyone who bothers to read notes; all manuscripts more recent in date than 1640 are, unless otherwise mentioned, still in the possession of the family.

Everything that is written hereafter has been attempt at truth. During the five centuries spent journeying from serfdom to squiredom, there have been many temptations and opportunities for the family to exaggerate its own importance. The author, being of bastard descent, has had to resist the subtler temptation to mock at the true worth of the Elmhirsts of Elmhirst.

EDWARD ELMHIRST

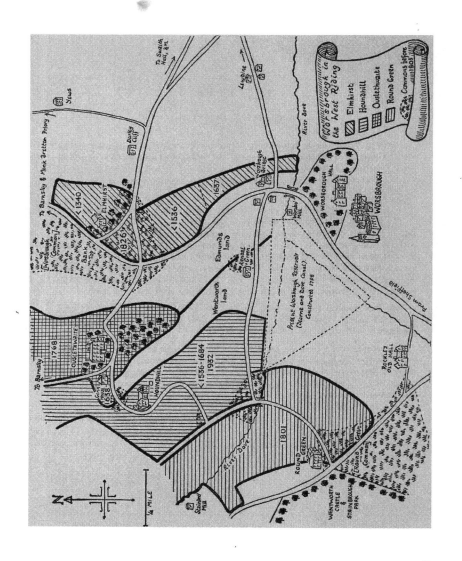

GENERATION I

ROBERT OF ELMHIRST
[Born before 1303, died between 1342 and 1360] ·

Six centuries ago the dale of Worsbrough was mostly woodland; on the slopes elm, ash and oak disputed for light with thick undergrowth of bramble and ivy; along the valley's lowest level willows and marshland lay with the twisting River Dove. The greater part of the dale with its river mill and its agricultural clearings belonged at this time, in the year 1340, to one of two Manors. The smaller portion to the west was still the property of a master who owned, in feudal style, the local manors of Rockley and Stainbrough. The larger eastern portion had been given a hundred years before by Clementia of Longvilliers, fearing for her soul, into the hands of the Catholic Church and the nuns of the great Cistercian Priory of Nun Appleton[1] lying far away near York.[2] The Prioress and her nuns had little personal contact with their property in Worsbroughdale and their steward probably came to the Dale only occasionally to hold Manor Courts and to collect rents and farm produce, it would be his duty to act as general supervisor, see that the necessary work was done and report to the Lady Prioress important matters which required her decision.

On a Monday morning, early in the winter of 1340, the local manor of Rockley was holding its court[3] and all the peasants had to be there early. Old Robert of Elmhirst[4] probably walked there from his clearing on the northern slope. First he would have passed beside the assarted, or newly-cleared, lands lately reclaimed from the forest's edge; closer to the manor lands lay the common fields and meadows which would have been well known to him, a few strips here and there would probably have been his own responsibility. The common fields were separated into these strips by ridges or baulks of raised turf.

Closer to the big house itself, in the Manor domain proper, Robert would be meeting and talking with other peasants called on the same business. The meeting-place was close to the manor buildings, probably in the barn or great hall of the house if it was raining. Since Rockley was not held by any absentee landlord or some impersonal religious establishment, the court was probably presided over by the lord himself; if he was busy or away from home the manor steward would take his place. Then, when all the weatherbeaten smelly peasants had collected, the steward called for silence, the clerk straightened out his long strip of vellum and began to record the proceedings. He headed it in his

---

[1] Grant confirmed by Henry III in 1249.
[2] Four miles east of Tadcaster.
[3] Rockley Court Roll. P.R.O. S.C.2 (Court Rolls).211.112.
[4] Until the fifteenth century was over, members of the family, in the Latin documents of the time, were always written "de Elmhirst" or the equivalent. It was and is incorrect to leave the "de" alone untranslated.

crabbed writing: "Court held at Rockley on the Monday next after the Feast of St. Martin-in-the-Winter[5] in the Year of Our Lord 1340." Then, when the roll-call was completed, the business of the morning began. Henry Cotes stood up and complained that William Harrison had been trespassing across his holdings; he produced a witness but the case was adjourned without a decision. Next came two peasants who had been having a dispute, probably recorded at earlier manor meetings, about a small debt; the plaintiff now admitted that he owed at least some of the money and was fined twopence for all the needless worry he had caused. John of Rockley, probably a servant who lived in the manor buildings, complained that John of the Woodhouse in the autumn of the year before, 1339, had come to a small wood, then held by the complainant, and cut down willows, oaks and other timber and caused a great deal of damage; John of the Woodhouse could not deny the evidence, some of the wood may indeed have been built into his nominal house: he admitted his guilt and the lord fined him fourpence.

Now came a long list of cases, always the commonest at Manor Courts, of peasants who had let their livestock roam into the lord's domain. Without hedges and fences, control must have been extraordinarily difficult and the peasant could only hope that the creature ate its moneysworth before being recognised or impounded. Robert of Wulthwaite, who had offered to be a witness in the first case to be called, had had his mare caught in the lord's domain last winter and was therefore fined fourpence. Our own Robert of Elmhirst was the next that had to stand forward; the steward reported that two of his farm horses had been caught roaming in the lord's meadow before Michaelmas, 1339; Robert knew he was guilty and the fine being fourpence, what he had anticipated for two horses, he put the silver on the clerk's desk and rejoined his friends.

Many more of Robert's neighbours had to be penalised before the long proceedings came to an end. John the son of Henry the Fisher,[6] had to pay two pence for two oxen straying in the same meadow near the manor hall. Isabel Woodhouse had let her cow wander into a field called Richard royd, when the harvest was ripening in the autumn of 1339, for the correspondingly larger damage to the lord's property she had to forfeit a shilling.

While the long roll of small offenders, jostling or queueing to pay their fines, went on, Robert of Elmhirst could talk quietly with his friends and learn all the local gossip; he himself was an old man and his strength was failing, but he could probably remember the time in his youth when serfs were serfs indeed. Nowadays things were easier and softer; the lord of the manor only occasionally demanded actual physical labour from his peasants and this was only particularly irritating at harvest-time when they had to leave their own common holdings,

---

[5] 11 November. (Two other St. Martin festivals share the winter.)
[6] Such a name as this, about this very time, could crystallise into either Harrison or Fisher.

just when they most needed attention, in order to help reap the grain from the lord's personal grounds and meadows. Robert of Elmhirst, the possessor of two farm horses, was a person of some consequence among his fellows and at times of forced labour would probably be expected to act as foreman or overseer among his less prosperous neighbours. The Lord of the Manor of Rockley, like lords of the manor all over England, had found it easier to allow serfs to pay money rents in the place of their own forced labour; more commonly still, rents were paid in the form of livestock. It was a peculiar period of transition most confusing to contemporary lawyers. A serf could own nothing; all he had, his hens, his money, his house and his very wife and children all belonged, like himself, to the lord of the manor. But there were obvious advantages in a more elastic system; a man would care more for his fields if he knew that after his retirement or death, they would be allowed to pass to his son; moreover, a contented peasant would not be so tempted to run away and leave the manor fields untilled. At this very court a man was admitted to the same fields that his father had farmed. John Fisher was called forward to do fealty for the lands that his father had relinquished; the ceremony usually consisted of kneeling before the steward, placing closed hands between the hands of the lord's representative and swearing the standard oath:

> "So help me God and all His Saints that from this day forth I shall be true and faithful to the Lord and shall owe fealty for the land which I hold of him in villeinage and that he may be justified of me in body and goods and that I shall not take myself off the Lord's Manor."[7]

In Fisher's case the steward was not certain under what traditional services the land was held and this was left to be settled at the next Manor Court. In the meantime there were three shillings to be paid for admittance into the paternal lands.

Isabel Woodhouse had been discovered brewing, probably barley left over from the last harvest. She had omitted to get the lord's permission and was lucky to get off with a warning. Since the last court meeting an old peasant named Wigfall had died. He had been busy assarting land in his last years, cutting back the forest's edge to carve out new fields. Clearings such as these were usually granted to younger sons who thus had land of their own to manage. Wigfall, however, had died before his son was of age sufficient to look after the assarted fields and therefore there was no alternative but for the lord to take Wigfall's clearings for himself, the land would then probably be leased out to other peasants until young Richard Wigfall was allowed to be old enough to take control.

A more serious matter came next. Two women had been quarrelling. Agnes of the town complained that the servant of Isabel Woodhouse, the unauthorised brewer who had been let off with a warning, had wounded and maltreated her, Agnes. Isabel confidently assured the court that Agnes was a

---

[7] H. S. Bennett. *Life on the English Manor*. Cambridge. 1938. p. 22.

liar. Then followed charge and counter-charge of trespass and it was probably all getting rather shrill when the steward saved himself by a technicality: since blood was alleged to have been spilt, he announced, the matter was too serious a one for the Manor Court to adjudicate and the decision would have to be made by the King's law. By way of anticlimax, a few minor matters remained to be settled before the proceedings were closed and the peasants were free to go about their own affairs.

Not many months after this Rockley Court, Robert of Elmhirst handed over the lands he farmed in Worsbrough Manor to his sons, when he had obtained permission from the authorities; the reason was almost certainly his increasing age and infirmity, by keeping control he would not be helping either himself or his family. It is known that old Robert had two grown-up sons. John, since he subsequently took over the greater part of the lands, can be assumed to be the firstborn. Richard, the second son, had a smaller share. In a pedigree compiled in 1638, which records this transaction, a third son, William, is named; though there is no proof that he existed, there is equally no evidence that he did not.

This transference of old Robert's lands, or rather, of the lands old Robert had been allowed to farm, is said to have occurred in 1341, and at the Manor Court of Worsbrough under the auspices of the steward of Nun Appleton Priory. These courts affected the early Elmhirsts much more intimately than did those held at Rockley, such as has just been described; the greater part of the family holdings were within the boundaries of Worsbrough Manor. When Clementia of Longvilliers left her lands there to Nun Appleton Priory in 1249, she bequeathed with the soil the peasants and what were subsequently translated as their "followers"[8]; the actual Latin is "*sequelae*," a word more accurately translated as "brood" or "litter". Whether Robert's grandparents were among these human livestock one unfortunately cannot tell. It seems likely that they were, their servile origin is clearly demonstrable in the succeeding centuries. Of this particular Manor Court of 1341 there is only as much known as was transcribed three hundred years later.[9] It is not alleged there that Robert was dead and in actual fact it is more probable that he was old and merely wanted to retire; a Robert of Elmhirst was still alive two years later[10] and this is likely to be the same man, furthermore it was quite common for an old peasant to see the property he had been farming transferred to a relative in the evening of his own lifetime and often there was agreement reached whereby the new tenant agreed to look after his aged parent. So it is very probable that Robert himself was present to see the property he knew so well being redistributed between his sons John and Richard.

---

[8] Exchequer Depositions. 1634. P.R.O. E. 134. 9 & 10 Chas. I. Hilary II.
[9] Worsbrough Manor Roll of 1341 quoted in Rich. Elmhirst's Pedigree of 1638.
[10] Rockley Court of 13 Dec., 1342. P.R.O. S.C.2 (Court Rolls) 211.112.

First John knelt and swore fealty for a messuage and "several lands and woods" in Worsbroughdale. In this particular manor, and many manors differed, the custom was that after paying fealty the new tenant was given token of his new holding by receiving a straw from the lord's steward; the custom survived at Worsbrough Manor Courts until late in the eighteenth century.

Richard, probably the younger son, was allowed to take control of other lands which had been tended by his father, a messuage and a bovate of land. A bovate, or an oxgang was, as its name suggests, the amount of land which could be ploughed by a single ox in one season; it varied in area, according to the soil and the system of tillage, between ten and eighteen acres. Fifteen acres would be an average bovate in the West Riding at this time. For this quantity of land, a handsome portion for a younger son, Richard did fealty to the steward and promised to pay the Lady Prioress a yearly tribute of three hens. William, if he was a son of Robert of Elmhirst, seems to have inherited no land.

It was the general rule that the holdings of peasants were not subdivided among their children. There was an obvious danger of the portions of land becoming insufficient for feeding the individual and his family, only those who held enough territory would be given their lord's permission to split the property. Old Robert of Elmhirst must have farmed some thirty acres of land on the Manor of Worsbrough, a few acres on the adjacent Manor of Rockley, and probably had, in addition, use of part of the woodlands in Worsbrough. The forest was hardly less useful than the land. Acorns, and there were many oaks among the trees there, were most valuable for feeding swine. Robert would not have had the right to cut wood when and where he wanted it, but manor custom allowed him to take fallen wood for fuel. Timber needed for the upkeep of houses could only be obtained with the lord's permission and by paying a fine. On some manors in Yorkshire the tenants were permitted to take, in addition to the fallen wood, dead branches sufficiently within reach to be dragged down by a crook—hence, "by hook or by crook."

In the management of his thirty acres, since they were part of the manorial grounds, Robert of Elmhirst would have had to farm in accordance with the general plan. The three-field system, which was the rule, entailed a rotation of crops. Ten acres would be sown with rye or wheat, the chief crop, another ten acres was planted with oats, barley, or vetches, and the third ten acres lay fallow. These last acres were used as grazing grounds and were consequently manured. The other twenty acres meanwhile had to be ploughed, the main function of Robert's trespassing horses, and then sown. The seed having been scattered by hand, the horses were again employed to drag the wooden harrow.[11] The harvest season was the hardest of all the year; not only had the peasants' own crops to be garnered by hand, and Robert must have been thankful for his

---

[11] H. S. Bennett. *Life on the English Manor*. Cambridge. 1938.

sons, but the stewards of the two manors would be perpetually demanding assistance to bring in the harvest from the fields in the lord's personal domains. Scythes cut all crops except wheat and for this a sickle was used. Five men as a rule could clear two acres in a day, so Robert would have had ten days to bring in his own harvest if only his manorial responsibilities could be finished or bought off. Tithes were generally collected directly from the fields and from the crop that was left had to be further deducted the seed for the next year and the payment of the fraction to the miller at the lord's mill on the side of the River Dove, where alone it was legal for the grain to be ground. Livestock would have been another source of profit, in addition to his horses Robert would have been certain to have had sheep, pigs, an ox or two, and an indeterminate number of agile hens.

After his retirement Robert, tied by a lifetime of habit, was likely to be seen pottering about the fields, helping his sons, talking perhaps of Crecy and the perpetual wars in France, but more probably, one thinks, entirely absorbed with local gossip and the doings of his neighbours. His youngest son[12] William was getting into trouble with the steward at Rockley Manor; he had been caught letting one of his animals graze on somebody else's fields. Young William claimed that he had an adequate answer to this charge and promised to bring a witness to support his story at the next meeting of the manor court; the steward obviously considered that William was temporising and since the accused had little or no land to act as security, the trespassing animal was impounded.[13] The next court was three months later[14] and, together with his young son, old Robert of Elmhirst then appeared for the last time. Young William's was the second case to be heard; the witness he had proposed to call was a servant who lived, presumably, in the manor buildings, but this ally failed to appear and William was subsequently fined twopence for the original offence. Robert of Elmhirst himself was not called until nearly the end of the day's business. Thomas, son of Beatrice, claimed that Peter of Rockley[15] had owed him two shillings and sixpence for a very long time, now he pressed for the payment of this, together with sixpence as interest or damages. Peter of Rockley "altogether contradicted" and because the sum was so large and because a criminal charge might be involved, the steward referred the case to the King's

---

[12] Or his nephew. See above and Appendix B.
[13] Rockley Court Roll, Sept. 1342. P.R.O. S.C.2 (Court Rolls) 211.112. Others penalised at the same court were Richard Simonson for making a pasture for himself and paying no dues on it to the lord, a peasant called Nicholas had made a path; another named Henry had tried to enclose a piece of the common lands and was therefore expelled from the commons; Peter Fisher kept a manure heap on the common and Hugh the German had cut a bundle of twigs in the lord's woods.
[14] Rockley Court Roll. Dec. 1342. P.R.O. S.C.2 (Court Rolls) 211.112. At this court the Bailiff, a peasant of Robert of Elmhirst's own status, was penalised because he had allowed people to trespass unchecked across the common lands. Richard the servant appeared too late to be of any help to young William Elmhirst and only to claim for himself a debt of fivepence which he said was owing to him from Hugh the German. At each of these courts a great deal of the business was concerned with trespassing livestock.
[15] Appearing at such a court this Peter is more likely to be a servant employed in Rockley Hall than a member of the gentle family of the lords of the manor.

Justice. Robert of Elmhirst, together with William Fisher, both being men of age and position, had their names recorded as pledges.

At the end of this manor court proceedings came a case of very real interest to everyone there. One of the worst grievances on all manors was the fact that all grain had to be ground in the mill which always belonged to the lord. The objections to this were many; there was always a waiting-list at the mill and the family was hungry.[16] There was nothing to ensure that the flour of doubtful quality handed back by the miller was really the produce of the harvest. Millers were notoriously both crafty and mean, often the place in the queue depended on the size of a cash present made to the man. Worst of all, perhaps, was that everyone, including the lord, knew exactly the size of everyone else's harvest and so knew exactly how much was liable to dues and taxation. Because of all these reasons it is not therefore surprising that for centuries peasants had been attempting to grind their own corn, making little stone hand-mills that could be worked discreetly in a back room, paying dues to nobody. John of Milnethorp and William Miller, both of whose fathers or grandfathers were probably millers who would be unlikely to spoil their own trade, had been concerned in the mass production of hand-mills and grinding stones. They had, in addition, adding insult to injury, got the stone for their hand-mills from under the lord's own land. During the preceding three months three pairs of grindstones, perhaps made by the same criminal pair, who had been caught red-handed with fifteen pairs of "gryndelstones," had been found in various houses within the manor boundaries. These were ordered to be confiscated and Miller and Milnethorp were fined forty pence for digging up the stone they had used and an additional four shillings and sixpence for making the finished products.

The end of this court meeting at Rockley, some day in the December of 1342, is the last known appointment of old Robert of Elmhirst. It seems likely that he died within the next few years.

---

[16] The manor mill, dependent on the sluggish Dove, must have been unconscionably slow in the autumn.

GENERATION II

RICHARD OF ELMHIRST
(Born before 1322, died between 1376 and 1379)

Though Richard was not the eldest son of Robert of Elmhirst, he is of more importance in this history because it is through him that the descent or ascent of the family is traced. Moreover, he appears to have been a successful man in the limited world to which he was born; his name recurs several times in the scanty records that have remained. John, the eldest brother, married and had a child that survived him, a daughter named Matilda.[1] Richard himself became married to a certain Alice[2] whose surname is unknown.

Very soon after he was admitted to his fifteen acres of land and the little house attached, there occurred one of the most appalling tragedies that ever came to England. The Black Death was to slaughter no less than one-third of the population and forever changed the lives of such men as Richard of Elmhirst.

The deadly epidemic, like the milder but more famous pestilence of 1665, was apparently bubonic plague; the fourteenth century Death seemed to have a particular liability to pulmonary complications. It came to England in the autumn of 1348, starting on the south coast and moving relentlessly northwards. In August the Archbishop of Canterbury died of it, the first of three so to perish. Forty days of indulgence were doled out to all who would pray that the visitation of God's anger should be averted. The winter between 1348 and 1349 made no difference to the awful mortality; this is understandable if the disease was indeed bubonic plague carried by infected rats; no better opportunity could be given the fleas to spread their bites among whole families, than in the long cold nights of winter when all the household was huddled close together in smoky, rat-infested shacks. By the January of 1349 the epidemic had spread to Bath and Exeter, in the early spring it was raging in London, and by the summer it burnt most fiercely in the Midlands, still moving steadily northwards until the autumn saw it at its worst in Yorkshire.

In the church at Worsbrough,[3] as elsewhere in the diocese and by the order of the Archbishop of York, there were processions and litanies and masses to be said every Wednesday and Friday for the staying of the pestilence. How little effective were these frightened shufflings and mumblings can be seen in the mortality figures of the local priesthood, the only body whose records were at

---

[1] Dodsworth MS. 155, folio 34. Bodleian Library.
[2] Poll Tax of 1379. P.R.O. Lay Subsidies. W. Riding. 206/49. Membrane 15b.
[3] Worsbrough "church" was indeed no church but a chapel dedicated to St. Mary, dependent on the parish church at Darfield.

all complete. In the Deanery of Doncaster thirty vicars or rectors died, from a total of fifty-six, in the fatal year.[4] Elsewhere it has been estimated that at least half of the clergy of Yorkshire perished in those dreadful times[5]; Meaux Abbey lost more than three-quarters of her monks and the Prior of Monk Bretton, the greatest local religious establishment lying close to Worsbrough, was himself a victim. Another neighbour, Thomas Allott of Wombwell, of a family much mated with the Elmhirsts, seeing the plague on every side of him and probably knowing himself to be stricken, asked in his will to be buried in Darfield and made his bequests with the proviso that his property was to go "to my sons and daughters living after this present mortal pestilence."

When the Black Death had burnt itself away, it was slowly realised that there had been a most fantastic and unexpected revolution; the lords of manors found their acres lying waste with none to till them; the peasants soon discovered that the value of their services had increased out of all expectation, the meek seemed likely to come to their inheritance. Nearly every commodity, and particularly food, had doubled in price. Various royal edicts were hustled out from Westminster, labourers were on no account to demand increases in pay and no employer was to raise wages in competition with others in the labour market; such regulations were quite worthless in the face of economic facts. Money had become the universal commodity and the old custom of paying rents by duties and farm produce began to disappear. Both peasant and landlord profited by the new arrangement, the peasant because his time and labour were now his own, the landlord because he obtained an economic factor of greater efficiency.[6] Hence it came about, when land lay cheap and empty in the years following the Death, that most of the wealthier serfs became, in addition to keeping their subordinate manorial status, also independent owners of personal lands of their own.

No Manor Court Rolls, either for Worsbrough or Rockley, remain from those chaotic years after the plague; nor even have any extracts survived. Indeed, it is very probable that no such records were ever made; when the world's doom was imminent a steward would hardly be anxious to record a trespass across deserted fields or the barren rooting of a hungry pig. Contemporary accounts of neighbouring Monk Bretton show that the arable lands belonging to the Priory went almost out of cultivation.[7]

Only one Elmhirst name, that of Richard, can be found both before and after the plague. Of old Robert, who may have died before, and of Richard's brothers, John and William, there is nothing to be found; it is no more than possible that they died in the Death.

[4] Hunter's *Deanery of Doncaster.*
[5] F. A. Gasquet. *The Black Death,* p. 231.
[6] P. Vinogradoff. *Villainage in England.* 1892, p. 181.
[7] J. W. Walker. *Monk Bretton Priory.* Y.A.S. 1926.

In the new world, when the hurricane had passed, Richard of Elmhirst flourished. His holdings in the Manors of Worsbrough and Rockley were doubtless increased by the respective lords, only too glad to find someone to keep their ground in cultivation. In return it is probable that other concessions were made, personal physical service was no more to be demanded, this and other humiliating stigmata of serfdom being finally converted into payment of regular cash rents; the only duty remaining was that of attendance at manor courts and what that involved by way of service on court juries and the filling of minor manorial offices.

A villein in Richard's position would be able to enter into valid civil contracts, to acquire property and to defend it against encroachment[8]; furthermore, such lands after the death of the villein would not normally come into the hands of the lord but would pass, as did the property of freemen, as the dead man had willed. In the autumn of 1358 Richard of Elmhirst was fined threepence for some minor offence at a Rockley Manor Court; unfortunately, this particular roll has had strips cut off it for some other purpose and no more can be discovered.[9] During these years his family was increasing and between the years 1357 and 1363 Alice, his wife, had a son John, and a daughter Joan.[10] In 1362 he again figured as an offender in the Manor Court of Rockley; this time it was the familiar old offence of allowing his animals to graze on the lord's pastures, he was fined fourpence.[11]

Next year, in November 1363,[12] he made his first recorded purchase of land that was to be his own personal property; in this case the land was very probably part of the waste acres in Worsbrough that had previously, before the plague, been worked by some villein who had perished. Richard did fealty in the Manor Court of Worsbrough to the representative of Idonea of Gainsborough, the Prioress of Nun Appleton, and she in return sent by the hand of the manor steward a release addressed to Richard and certified with the manor seal.[13] By another charter of about the same time he got possession of an assart of land from the sisters Went, this land however was merely for occupation during his lifetime.[14] In four more years he was again buying land, from a certain Robert of the Cliff,[15] for this land, too, he undoubtedly would have had to do fealty to the Lord of the Manor, not servile fealty as bondmen paid, but an oath of loyalty such as, at the top of the feudal tree, the King would have expected of his barons.

[8] P. Vinogradoff. *Villainage in England.* 1892, p. 67.
[9] Rockley Court Roll. 21 Sept. 1358. P.R.O. Court Rolls. S.C.2. 211.113.Memb.1.
[10] Poll Tax of 1379. P.R.O. Lay Subsidies 206/49. Membrane 15b.
[11] Rockley Court Roll. 25 Oct. 1362. P.R.O. Court Rolls. S.C.2. 211.113. Membrane 3b.
[12] Pedigree Roll of 1638 quoting Worsbrough Court Roll of 20 Nov. 1363.
[13] Such a Release conveyed an estate where the grantee, Richard, was already in possession.
[14] After his death the land was to go to a John Went unless John should be childless when Richard was able to leave it to his own heirs. (Dodsworth MS. 53, undated, Bodleian.) The Prior of neighbouring Monk Bretton between 1323 and 1338 also had the unusual name of Went. (J. W. Walker. *Monk Bretton Priory.*)
[15] Pedigree of 1638 quoting Worsbrough Court Roll of St. Martin's day, 1367.

On two more occasions Richard features in the Rockley Manor Rolls,[16] in 1372 and 1376.[17] Both parchments are in such poor condition that little more than the name can be deciphered.

At the time of his death, which occurred within the next three years, the family fortunes were in a flourishing state; to the fifteen and more acres that he held by custom of the manors of Worsbrough and Rockley, he had added the other lands he had bought, in a countryside still underpeopled, with his own money.

---

[16] Rockley Court Roll. P.R.O. Court Rolls. S.C.2. 211 No. 113. Membs. 8 & 11b.

[17] It may be that this Richard was the son of the last Richard. The reason being that in 1369 Robert, possibly another son, was known as Robert the son of Alice which he would not have been called if Alice's husband was still alive.

GENERATION III

JOHN OF ELMHIRST
(Born between 1357 and 1363, probably died 1429)

The affairs of the nation must have been of very little interest or weight in a remote Yorkshire dale in mediaeval times, yet on one occasion the undistinguished inhabitants of Worsbrough were affected in a way as unpleasant for them as it is fortunate for the genealogist. The perpetual wars in France were going badly as the English lost their aggressiveness and became mere garrisons. Young Richard of Bordeaux, affected and extravagant, frittered away the conquests of his father and grandfather. To raise more money that he might control his unpleasant uncles, the French, the Scots and his elegant courtiers, device was now had to a Poll Tax.

Every adult in the kingdom, excepting only the paupers and genuine beggars, had to pay a capital levy according to their social status. These amounts varied from eighty shillings for an English Earl down to fourpence "for each married man, for him and his wife, who are not of the beforementioned position [*i.e.*, of higher social status], over the age of sixteen years, excluding bona-fide mendicants," and fourpence too was the tax for "each unmarried man and woman over the age of sixteen."

By no means all these polls, which give a valuable census of the population, have survived. That for the West Riding is, however, in the Public Record Office and here, for the township of Worsbrough, are recorded among their neighbours:

Alice of Elmerst	4d.
John her son	4d.
Joan her daughter	4d.

This entry shows that by this year, 1379, not only was Richard probably dead, but that two at least of his children were over sixteen years of age, alive and unmarried. In the neighbouring township of Cawthorne there lived a Robert and Beatrice of Aylmeherst with their unmarried grown-up daughter; if this name is equivalent to Elmhirst, the relationship with the main line is not known but this may be the same Robert, son of Alice Elmyrste, who had been granted land in Hoyland Swain by John Catelyn in 1369[1] and it is possible that he was an elder son of the widow Alice, who was being taxed in Worsbrough.

When the tenant of land on a manor died before his son and heir came of

---

[1] Dodsworth MS. 62, folio 14 (Bodleian). On the same folio is another, undated, deed by which John the son of Thomas Davy of Hoyland Swain, gave and quit claimed to Robert "le Tayllour", son of John "de Elmenhirst", lands in Hoyland Swain.

age, the practice varied in different places. The rule in Worsbrough at this time was for the widow to be allowed to take control of all her late husband's lands on condition that their eldest son was admitted tenant when he reached his majority. It is likely, therefore, that Alice, at the time of the Poll Tax, held Elmhirst in her own name; a few years later, in 1384, at the latest, John would have taken over from her by some arrangement satisfactory to his mother, to himself and, most important of all, the steward of the manor. With the freehold lands that his father had acquired John's method of inheritance would depend absolutely on his father's last will.

Regarding John's relations at this time there must be considerable doubt. He may well have had two elder brothers, Richard who died young, and possibly Robert of Cawthorne. He certainly had a cousin Matilda, who had married Roger Genn, and there was another cousin, William, the son of his other kinsman William.[2] John's cousin William was priest[3] and vicar of Bolton-on-Dearne between 1401 and 1403, when he resigned and disappeared from the records;[4] the advowson of Bolton was the property of Monk Bretton Priory, which lay so close to Worsbrough; the payments due to the parish priest automatically went to the Priory, which was then responsible for appointing and paying a vicar. The monks made a profit out of this arrangement, the rectory was worth £30 5s. 8d. annually to the Priory, which only paid out £6 13s. 4d. to the incumbent whom they appointed.[5] The selection of William Elmhirst as vicar does not necessarily mean that he was a monk at Bretton though such a selection from among his own monks was usually made by the Prior.

About the year 1409,[6] John's other cousin, Matilda Genn, appeared in Worsbrough Manor Court to claim tenancy of lands which had hitherto been occupied by William, the son of William, the son of John Elmhirst. At this same court, Matilda and her husband, Roger Genn, paid five shillings as merchet: this was the fine paid to the lord of the manor at the marriage of a female serf and represented compensation to him for the loss of the woman's services. "There is no service in the world," emphasised Justice Belknap in 1342, "which so quickly proves a man to be a villein as making a fine for marriage."[7]

No less significant is the next disaster, enveloped in complications both genealogical and social. The Worsbrough Manor Rolls, sometime in the

---

[2] In May 1386, Sir Robert and Elizabeth Rockley leased lands unspecified to William Elmhirst at a yearly rent of 6s. 8d. (MS. Dodsworth 139, folios 28 and 28b.)

[3] Probably the same priest, "Sir" William of Elmhirst, had land in Bolton claimed from him by Thomas of Hemsworth and others. 8 June 1380.

[4] MS. of James Torre (1649-1699). York Minster Library.

[5] J. W. Walker. Monk Bretton Priory. Y.A.S. 1926.

[6] MS. Dodsworth 155, folio 34. The proceedings are dated 18 April, "the tenth year of King Henry". Henry IV is almost certainly correct, at his accession no other king of the name had reigned within living memory. The numbers of the Henries who immediately succeeded him would not be thus omitted.

[7] H. S. Bennett. Life on the English Manor, p. 240. This payment of merchet was not transcribed by newly-rich Richard Elmhirst in his 1638 pedigree and, more shamefully, it was again ignored two hundred years later, when a haughty pedigree was written for Burke's "Landed Gentry".

fourth year of the reign of Henry IV (1402 or 1403) contained an entry that: "One William the son of William Elmhirst, the Lord's villein, was fled or escaped forth of the said Manor of Worsbrough." An order was recorded in the same Roll that the Court Guard was to apprehend him and bring him to his judgment.[8] This entry, which must be believed both because of the respectability of the two men who claimed to have read it, and because it was never challenged, cannot be reconciled with the recorded pedigree.[9]

A villein could find freedom in one of three ways, all of which seem to have been adopted at different times by different Elmhirsts. A serf might buy his liberty, or he might become a priest, or lastly he might seek liberty in flight as did this hunted William. Running away was no light undertaking, a final and irrevocable act fit only for a young man without a family. Friends and relatives, the sure, slow, settled life in the valley, all had to be left forever and exchanged for doubtful advantages in strange surroundings. Most such runaways as William fled to the nearest town, where they could work at odd jobs until a year and a day had elapsed and they were technically no longer classed as bondmen. Sometimes they might go to live on some distant manor, perhaps even buying land with money they had been hoarding. If ever they were foolish enough to return to visit relatives or acquaintances in the manor from which they had fled, they were considered to have returned to their "villeins' nest" and were liable to instant arrest.

A legitimate road of escape lay through the schoolhouse to the priesthood. If a child could be taught to read and write, he became a clerk or cleric, inside the pale of the church he was what was popularly called a "bondman of Christ", having exchanged his earthly lord for the heavenly Lord; priests by virtue of their calling owed service to no human being. Education as a method of escape became increasingly popular among the unfree and correspondingly disliked by the proud free-born clerics. Langland's bitter scorn can still be appreciated: "Bondsmen's children have been made bishops, and men's bastards have been archdeacons." About this time the King was petitioned that he would forbid presumptuous villeins from sending their brats to school; in 1406, to his great credit and against the advice of both noblemen and highborn prelates, he refused. Nevertheless, the lords of manors, though they might not be able to forbid schooling, could discourage it by heavily fining ambitious parents: a young man that entered the church was a great loss to the manor, not only was his personal service and manual productivity lost, but his subsequent childlessness meant further incalculable damage to the revenue of the estate. Probably towards

---

[8] Roll quoted by Thos. Hanson and Thos. Oke in *Rich. Elmhirst* v. *The Hansons*, 1626.

[9] William, John's uncle, would probably not have had two sons named William. One, the vicar, and one the runaway. Neither would a vicar ever be described as an official villein nor would a vicar be likely to have an official son. Various attempts can be made to explain this multitude of William Elmhirsts praying, begetting, dying without heirs and fleeing from the manor. A partial but not unlikely solution is that the runaway William was never recaptured, his father William, therefore, when he came to die about 1409, had no *available* heir and his lands on the manor were then claimed by his kinswoman Matilda, who represented the senior line.

the end of the fourteenth century, other Elmhirsts sought thus to escape. There remains the evidence that:

> "it doth also appear by the said Court [Rolls] that some of [Elmhirst's] name or generation have been reported, used or esteemed as villeins or bondmen of the Manor [of Worsbrough] and fined forty pence for putting his sons to school without licence, and his daughters [were] recorded as bondwomen."[10]

It seems most likely that this unnamed offender would be either Richard's brother William (whose son William later became a priest and thus justified his education), or the John now under consideration, who had more than one son.

When John grew old he came to a similar arrangement with a son as his grandfather seems to have done. On the marriage of his elder son, John, with a certain Margaret, John Elmhirst senior granted, as far as he was able, the land at Elmhirst itself and other lands in addition, doubtless Richard's purchases, to his son John Elmhirst junior. In exchange for this concession, the younger man promised his father a certain rent for the remainder of his life.[11]

---

[10] Evidence of Thos. Oke in *Richard Elmhirst v. The Hansons*, 1626.
[11] Richard Elmhirst's Pedigree Roll of 1638.

GENERATION IV

WILLIAM ELMHIRST
(Born about 1415, died probably 1485)

John and William[1] were the two sons of the last John and young John at least, as had been seen, was grown up at the time that his father was going into retirement. This John, the elder brother, is of interest chiefly because through him the privately acquired lands probably passed out of the family possession. As regards the land held in the manor, as a descendant wrote in 1638:

"Our family as I conceive assumed their surname from a messuage in Worsbroughdale in the County of Yorke, which now ys and for many ages hath beene, our peculiar Inheritance and doth not appear by any evidence that I could ever yet see to have been the Inheritance of any other Family."[2]

This claim that the manor lands, Elmhirst in particular, have always been held by the family certainly seems to be true. In 1409 a John Elmhirst of Elmhirst occupied the property, because on the 16th April of that year, Robert of Pilley conceded to him by deed two patches of ground assarted from the forest or from the waste lying to the north of Elmhirst.[3] This John may have been either John senior (then aged about fifty and unlikely to be taking on further responsibilities), or John junior, still sufficiently youthful to imagine he could manage anything, even the waiting weeds in the forest's edge. This 1409 record was used in more recent times when attempts were made to ennoble ancient lineage at the cost of veracity. From being simply the "Occupier of Elmhirst," which is all John would have been allowed to consider himself, he is translated into "lord of Elmhirst", which is something he never was; the land was only held by the will of the lord of the Manor of Worsbrough and three hundred and eighty years later honest Elmhirsts were willing to admit this in the manor court.[4] An interesting point about this deed of 1409 is that it shows that the original clearing in the forest which had been made by Elmhirsts, who had probably emigrated from the purlieu of the manor house, was now being augmented by the inclusion of more of the light soil lands in that area, which had been cleared by men of another family.[5]

Perhaps the elder brother of this generation, John, who died without children, had better be put out of the story first. By good fortune and a subsequent lawsuit,[6] contested before the original Worsbrough Court Rolls were

---

[1] The relationship of this William cannot be shown by evidence from contemporary documents.
[2] Elmhirst is certainly unique both as a place and a name; there has never been a surname Elmhurst, but several places are so called, a London laundry and an Irish mental home, in addition to innumerable villas.
[3] Pedigree Roll of 1638.
[4] Worsbrough Court Roll. 27 Dec. 1790.
[5] Appendix K.
[6] *Rich. Elmhirst* v. *The Hansons*, 1626.

destroyed, a considerable amount can be discovered about this barren branch of the tree. In the eighth year of Henry VI, 1429 or 1430, John paid a fine to the lord on entering into his father's lands on the manor. It is reasonable to presume that this year the father died and John junior came into the remainder of the lands, part of which he had already obtained by agreement. He enjoyed his father's lands for no more than a year because in another court held at Worsbrough in 1430 or 1431, his wife Margaret took over her husband's lands. The only occurrence that would have made this permissible was the death of her husband (if flight from serfdom or mental deficiency can safely be excluded).

Confirmation that Margaret was indeed left as a young widow was found in another court entry two years later, 1432 or 1433, when the Elmhirst lands which she had held in the meanwhile were surrendered to the lord because of her impending remarriage. Her new husband was a George Tingle; widows who found second husbands could be a nuisance on a manor, if they married a man outside the manorial jurisdiction they might try to take themselves away from the manor and leave their fields neglected. On the other hand, the husband might move into the widow's lands and such a foreigner, full of strange farming ways and often of doubtful manorial status, could be a disruptive influence in the midst of the traditional organisation. In earlier mediaeval days widows could only marry a suitor of whom the lord approved, but by the time that Margaret was getting a second husband she would probably not be penalised for remarriage, except perhaps for the routine merchet. Her new husband would himself pay his fine if the lands in question, which the widow had automatically forfeited on marriage, were regranted to him as her new husband.

By Margaret's marriage to Tingle a great deal of family property was lost, most of it being privately owned lands acquired in the halcyon half-century for villeins that followed the Black Death. The lands held of the manor, Elmhirst in particular, seem to have been automatically regranted by the lord of the manor to the next eldest male Elmhirst, in this case dead John's brother William.[7]

Three hundred years ago, when the family pedigree was first written, a great deal more could be said besides the bald facts that William Elmhirst married someone called Alice and had a son Robert. His will, dated 1472, was still extant in those days[8] but is not now to be found. It would not have been destroyed with the Worsbrough Manor Rolls, because it was naturally not the lands that he held of the manor that he could bequeath to anyone; the very fact of there having been a will at all suggests that he had acquired some land in his own right.[9]

[7] A comparable situation was to arise in 1684 when, an Elmhirst heiress marrying "out of the Manor", Elmhirst and the other lands were received back by the lord of the manor and regranted to the senior male Elmhirst.

[8] Pedigree Roll of 1638.

[9] This William is likely to have been the Willm. Helmyrst who was among the witnesses of the will of Robert Rockley. 11 Feb. 1448. (York Probate Registry, vol. 2, folio 189.)

Though William's will was dated 1472, he seems not to have died for another thirteen years. The Worsbrough Manor Rolls showed that in 1485 Alice, his widow, was admitted tenant to the lands that had previously been occupied by her husband.[10] There is no way of telling whether this admittance was to a widow's portion or to the whole; if the latter it would be safe to assume that her son Robert was a minor. However since at the time of his death William must have been an old man and since Robert his son was to die some thirty years after his father, it is probable that this admittance was merely to her widow's share of the manorial holdings of her late husband.

---

[10] *Richard Elmhirst* v. *The Hansons.* P.R.O., C21. E 19.8. Evidence of Thos. Hanson.

GENERATION V

ROBERT ELMHIRST
(Born about 1450, died about 1519)

Less is known about this Robert, the fifth generation since the history began, than of any of the other human links in the chain. No manor Rolls, either of Worsbrough or Rockley, remain. Perhaps the wars of York and Lancaster may have interfered with the regular accounts, possibly the Worsbrough Manor records, being held by the Priory of Nun Appleton, were destroyed in the social revolution which overturned the religious orders and broke the monasteries; the more recent records would have been taken away for study by those in charge of the dissolution of the Nunnery when they were trying to calculate revenues.

It is known that Robert Elmhirst married a Margaret. Her maiden name may possibly have been Seyll; this is mere conjecture based on the fact that in her will two Seylls receive bequests while the other legatees are all relations of her husband. Robert and Margaret had a large family of five sons and three daughters, details given in the pedigree of 1638[1] must be accepted here.

The eldest child, Robert, died very young and his name was subsequently given to another of the sons. Henry and the second edition of Robert died childless, Henry as a grown man and Robert perhaps as unfortunate as his namesake. Two more of the sons grew to manhood, James a priest, and William, born the fourth son, promoted by death to second place and by the Roman Church to priority; ultimately the only continuer of the line. Both the daughters, Agnes and Margery, married locally; Agnes to a Benson, and Margery to Roger Genn, of Ouslethwaite.

Robert's eldest surviving son, James, who entered the priesthood, remains both a theoretical credit and a certain mystery. He was described some hundred years after his death as

"the personablest priest in that Age, Crossbearer to Cardinal Thomas Wolsey Archbishop of York, Legate de Latere, and Chancellor of England; after the Cardinal's death the said James was parson of St. Swithen's in London."[2]

None of this can be confirmed, but it remains not unreasonable except for the fact that the period's "personablest priest" could live and die so unnoticed by his contemporaries. All that is known of this James is that in December 1517, he was ordained an acolyte and thence by stages of sub-deacon and deacon he became Priest in just under a year.[3] During this first twelve-month, the

---

[1] Richard Elmhirst's pedigree roll of 1638.
[2] Pedigree Roll of 1638.
[3] Information from Dr. Purvis, York Diocesan Archivist.

only part of his life that can be traced, he was at Nun Appleton, probably as Chaplain.

Wolsey had several crossbearers, but search through contemporary state papers reveals the name of only one, and he is another Yorkshireman, a Pilkington.[4] On Wolsey's appointment as Archbishop of York, several local crossbearers were probably appointed; the Minster records give no evidence. Then as his pomp grew equal to that of the king himself, the numbers of his retinue enormously increased; just before the Cardinal's fall, in October 1529, this army of household retainers and hangers-on were eating 430 oxen and 200 sheep a month[5]; perhaps it is not really so surprising that a country-born cross-bearer should be elbowed into obscurity.

Concerning James's second appointment, that of parson to St. Swithin's in London, the evidence is again rather negative, in spite of the fact that the church seemed to have had Yorkshire connections and Yorkshire benefactors. The church records were destroyed in the Great Fire, together with the building itself; ecclesiastical records at Lambeth and elsewhere have no record of any such Rector.[6]

The only writing that remains concerning the undistinguished Robert himself, the father of James the priest, and of Henry and William, is to be found in the Probate Registry of York, where:

"On the 5th day of October 1519 it was ordered that the Probate of the Will of Robert Elmehirste late of Darfelde in the Diocese of York deceased be exhibited before the feast of St. Martin next."[7]

There is, however, no record of any such will having been proved and the only deduction that can be drawn from this evidence is that Robert died in or before 1519.

---

[4] Among debts owing to Wolsey, 23 Oct., 21 Hen. 8, is one from John Pilkington, "One of My Lord's crossbearers". (State Papers Domestic, Henry VIII.)

[5] State Papers, Domestic, Henry VIII.

[6] Walter Stone was Rector there from 1504 till his resignation in 1518. Richard Parker was appointed as chaplain from 27 Aug. of that year and remained in office until his death in Feb. 1534. From Feb. 1534 to 1548, Richard Chaterton was Rector. It is conceivable that James Elmhirst was absentee rector during Parker's chaplaincy. (Novum Rep. Eccles. Parochiale Londiniense. Collection by George Hennessy, 1898.)

[7] Doncaster Act Book.

GENERATION VI

WILLIAM ELMHIRST
[1480-1560]

About 1519, when their father died, James, the eldest brother, was probably about to start his cross-carrying for the Cardinal in his see of York. The second brother, Henry, remained in Worsbrough, but does not appear to have married or had any children. William, the youngest son, married someone called Agnes Hall, who came from Smithley, a farm at the east end of Worsbroughdale, and doubtless spent most of his time working in the fields for his relations.

Their old mother, Margaret, was still living and, like most Elmhirst widows, was destined to stay alive longer than might have seemed strictly necessary. Perhaps she dwelt with bachelor Henry. She remained in nominal control until 1546 and in this period the value of her properties increased by nearly half. In one Lay Subsidy Roll of the fifteenth year of Henry VIII (1523 or 1524)[1] she is listed as Uxor Helmhirst and her goods are valued at £5; the following year she is recorded as Margareta Helmehirst.[2] In the former days the widow of a bond-tenant had usually inherited all her dead husband's lands, but the custom was changing in early Tudor days, bond-tenants were beginning to be described as copyhold tenants and widows were more frequently being allowed only a third part of the property while the son and heir was granted the remainder. It is certain from the Subsidy Rolls and her will that in this case the old woman owned both livestock and farming equipment, but the latter document also shows that Henry had at least a small flock of sheep. The dissolution of the monasteries, the inevitable outcome of social change and religious reformation, took place in the years immediately after 1536. King Henry VIII was nominally heir to all possessions of the Church; commissioners were set to work listing monastic properties and their rents to ensure that their royal master should not be cheated of his inheritance. These lists of places and rentals survive; two are of particular interest here. Monk Bretton Priory was the biggest of all the local establishments, but chanced to own little property in Worsbrough itself; most of the land there had been bequeathed over the centuries and by the vagaries of deathbed repentances to distant Nun Appleton.

Monk Bretton, lying like a whale to the north-east, floundered and died shortly before Nun Appleton was overwhelmed, Bretton's fat was rendered down under the expert eyes of the infamous Commissioners, Layton and Legh. They arrived at the monastery in February 1536, travelling in some state and accompanied by eight liveried servants. The Prior and thirteen monks attended

---

[1] Public Record Office. Lay Subsidies. E.179. 207/129.
[2] Public Record Office. Lay Subsidies. E.179. 206/113.

them in the Chapter house where enquiries were made into sources of income, relics of superstition and vices. The annual income was about £325, super-stitious relics were absent, but sodomy and incest were listed among the vices. Though so close and so powerful, this priory got only 4 per cent. of its income from Worsbroughdale and Penistone combined; a mediaeval Rockley seeking salvation had left the monks a bovate of land at Swaith, together with his mortal remains; an earlier Rockley three hundred years before the dissolution had given the Priory two acres in return for prayers for his dead parents.[3] The monks themselves were not badly treated, they were allowed to share the library, the Prior bought thirty-one books, while the lesser brethren took almost another hundred books between them.[4] They were all given pensions, the Prior had an annuity of £40 and the thirteen monks retired with £76 a year among them.[5] This comparatively generous treatment, which was not denied to those accused of immorality, was probably due to the fact that the Prior and the monks, seeing the end to be inevitable, had surrendered their house volun-tarily to the King's agents.

The fall of Nun Appleton, which had owned the greater part of Worsbrough for close on three centuries, was not to be long delayed; the same business men, Layton and Legh, the dissolution-mongers, arrived one autumn at Appleton to enquire into the records, the relics of superstition and more ladylike vices. The inevitable order of dissolution followed the surrender of Nun Appleton on 5th December 1540, and the lands passed to the King: for a long while the effects of the change were not apparent, the same steward, retained because he knew local conditions, might still come to collect the same fines. Perhaps he was later to be replaced by a cleverer man from London, who would be easier to swindle.

The Crown very quickly disposed of thousands of acres of newly acquired property; some were distributed among favourites at a favoured price, while a great deal more was sold through intermediaries and on the open market.[6] The new commercial middle-class, carried upwards by trade and traffic beyond the seas, gained lands of their own, pushing themselves among the few anaemic remnants of the ancient aristocracy, all that had been left from the bloody wars of York and Lancaster. The Elmhirsts sadly missed their opportunity. Henry and his mother bought no land and William, a younger son with a growing family, cannot have had much money. Their brother James, then parson of St. Swithin's, must have died about the time of the dissolutions. One almost

---

[3] J. W. Walker. *Monk Bretton Priory.* Y.A.S., 1926. The last of these Rockley bequests may have been part of Kendal Green, which lies adjacent to the Rockley properties. The Crown held this property from the time of the dissolutions until Roger Elmhirst bought it in 1575.

[4] Joseph Wilkinson. *Worsborough: Its Historical Associations and Rural Attractions.* Barnsley [1872], p. 382. This little book has been of great use in compiling this history. References to it hereafter will be under the title *Hist. Wors.*

[5] Rowland Jackson. *History of Barnsley.* 1858, p. 240.

[6] Nun Appleton, or half of it, was granted to Sir William Fairfax. Nun Appleton Hall was built there by Thomas Lord Fairfax.

hopes he died before; as churchman and professional crossbearer, he would not have appreciated the merits of the reformed religion.

In 1545 or 1546 the old dame who had so long been in nominal control of the copyhold estates began cautiously to admit her grown-up sons to their responsibilities. In the Lay Subsidy Tax of that period she is listed, as had been done before, as Uxor Helmhirst, with taxable goods valued at £7.[7] In another subsidy of the same year she appears again as Uxor Helmhyrst, but now, lower down on the list, very much lower, are William Helmhurst and Henry Helmhyrst, worth fortypence each of which twopence is lost in the tax.[8] In 1547 she is still in nominal charge.[9]

William's elder brother Henry and his mother both died about 1551: the son must have died first because in her will his mother makes a bequest of "all the sheep that did belong to my son Henry Elmhirste", since the will was proved soon afterwards there would not be more than the span of a sheep's life between the two family deaths. Even after Henry's death, William would not have been in a much improved financial position if all the copyhold lands were held by his ancient mother. In her will, which has already been mentioned, she asked to be buried at Worsbrough. Most of her property naturally was left to her son, four oxen were to come to him immediately and two other oxen later, by paying in one case thirteen shillings and fourpence and in another "the price of the said ox at the sight of two honest men", all the farming equipment that the oxen were to drag, "wains, ploughs and harrows belonging to husbandry" also came to him, together with her best blue gown, doubtless intended for his wife Agnes.

Henry's sheep were to go to "little William", no surname is mentioned, but a reasonable guess is that this might be the first-born son of William and one that never lived to maturity. The testator's other grandson, Roger, and her grand-daughter Agnes each had a cow, as did William's two married sisters, Agnes (Benson) and Margery (Genn). Coverlets and sheets were left to three people, among whom figures Henry Seyll. An Agnes Seill got six shillings and eightpence: Seyll, or Seill, is not a Worsbrough name and these, as already mentioned, may very well be relatives of the old woman's own family.[10] This will, which is dated 17th March 1551, was proved on 6th October of the year following by her son William, who from this time onwards was the head of the family.[11] He was admitted tenant the same year to the ancestral holdings of Bank Top (or Elmhirst) and Houndhill.[12]

[7] P.R.O. Lay Subsidies. E.179. 207/195.
[8] P.R.O. Lay Subsidies. E.179. 207/192.
[9] P.R.O. Lay Subsidies. E.179. 208/207.
[10] Katherine Seyll, whose will was proved 16 Oct. 1551, lived near Ripon. Nicholas Sayll, from somewhere near Doncaster, had his will proved 28 Jan. 1557. (York Probate Registry, vol. 13, folio 87, and vol. 15 (2), folio 185, respectively.) Neither will gives any hint of relationship to Elmhirsts.
[11] York Probate Registry, vol. 13, folio 915.
[12] Evidence of John Jackson, *Roger Elmhirst* v. *Richard Beckett*, 1588.

Like so many of his line, William, when he grew old, arranged for his son to take control of the copyhold property before they came to him by death. This transaction had the Manor sanction in 1556 or 1557[13] and the old man was still alive three years later.

In the summer of 1560, now with more time on his hands, he played an important part in promoting local education at this period when grammar schools were being founded all over the country. He and a neighbour called Broddesworth applied to the Manor Court that they might jointly be admitted copyhold tenants to a small plot of land lying across the road from Worsbrough Church, on which they intended to have a schoolmaster's house built.[14] This land was granted to them and their heirs at the rent of fourpence a year by the Crown agents, in whom the manor was now vested. In the same court, it is difficult to understand for what reason, old William and his colleague handed the copyhold, with permission, to fourteen other trustees, all local inhabitants, headed by Esquire Robert Rockley, and including in their number "Roger Elmehirst son & heir apparent of the sayd William". All these men and their heirs were made joint copyhold tenants of the same piece of land "To the use profitt & behoofe of one Syr Willm. Wolley, clerke, nowe a Scolemayster & teacher of Scollers at Worsbrough" for his lifetime or for as long as he was able and diligent in his teaching and after him for the use of his successors, who were to be elected by the majority of the board. A paragraph is added which would permit the trustees to dismiss Sir William or any subsequent holder of the office for negligence if there was no improvement after preliminary cautioning.[15] The Schoolmaster was called "Syr" William, as a mark of respect to his clerkship, a late example of the practice of so calling all priests in the Middle Ages.[16] Woolley may well have been a remnant of a local dissolved monastery, but if this was the case, he would probably have to have turned from his ancient faith before he would be permitted to teach impressionable youth.[17]

This fleeting appearance of old William Elmhirst is the last record that remains of him, alive or dead. There is no record of his burial in Worsbrough although the parish register had now been started.[18] As with other villages, the state of the earliest records was more a register of the education and enthusiasm of the parson or the parish clerk than a strict account of births, deaths and marriages. The death or burial of his widow Agnes is recorded in the register as on 26 July 1577.

---

[13] *Roger Elmhirst* v. *Richard Beckett*, 1588.
[14] And where the Schooldame's house still stands.
[15] Copy of Worsbrough Court Roll, presumably that held by the trustees, dated 12 June, 2 Eliz., in the vestry of Worsbrough Church.
[16] As with Sir William of Elmhirst in 1380, *vide supra*, Gen. III.
[17] Richard Hinchcliffe, alias Woolley, was a monk at Monk Bretton before the Dissolution and bought some of the Priory books. (Hunter's *South Yorkshire*, II, 274.)
[18] In 1558.

GENERATION VII

Roger Elmhirst of Houndhill and Elmhirst
[1520]-1594

When Roger took over the copyhold lands from his father, the family that existed, apart from his parents and wife, were his two sisters, now probably married—Agnes to John Forster, and Janet to John Cawood, who lived at Rob Royd in Worsbrough.

Confirmation of the transference of the copyhold before his father's death is found in a law suit which Roger had thirty years later,[1] when a Worsbrough Court Roll was shown, dated "the third and fourth years of Philip and Mary" (1556-1557), where he is mentioned as having been admitted tenant "of certain messuages, land and closes held of the Manor by copyhold."[2] This is the earliest local use of the word copyhold by which this form of customary tenure was later known. The phrase is self-explanatory; the tenant could show no proof of his right to the lands except by producing a copy of the Court Roll by which he was admitted to the holdings of his ancestors.

As Roger established himself at Houndhill and Banktop, or Elmhirst, with his newly-married wife Elizabeth, the daughter of Thomas Marsh, of the Dairy House at Darton, there was nothing to show that he would accelerate the upward movement of the family fortunes.[3] Others before him had inherited the right to farm these same lands and had been content so to do till they in their turn were underneath the church across the valley.

Roger was not to spend his life watching oxen steaming ahead of him across the ploughland. The slow creatures disappeared, giving place to jostling sheep; ploughlands became pastures. This radical change in his farming probably took some years to complete and does not seem to have been part of a general process in the neighbourhood, though the monks at Monk Bretton Priory to the north of the dale had been breeding them in the first quarter of the fourteenth century and by 1340 had made a fulling mill and dam on the river Dearne.[4] Roger's sheep were primarily raised for their wool and not their meat. They were sheared at Houndhill and elsewhere; there, too, the entire processes of cloth-making and dyeing were undertaken. The weaving mill still survived in the twentieth century.

Very soon after he was admitted to the copyhold lands, Roger and Elizabeth had their first child. The baby, Robert, was baptised at Worsbrough on

---

[1] *Roger Elmhirst* v. *Richard Beckett.* 11 Sept. 1588. Evidence of John Jackson. P.R.O. Exchequer Proceedings.
[2] The first mention of closes, implying sheep.
[3] His possessions are rated at only £3 in the Lay Subsidy of 1568 (Public Record Office. E.179. 208/241.)
[4] J. W. Walker. *Monk Bretton Priory.* Y.A.S. 1926.

13 January 1559-1560, and is recorded at the beginning of the church register. In the next years a large family arrived, three more sons, John [1564], William (1572), Roger,[5] and six daughters—Elizabeth, Joan, Margaret, Agnes, Mary and Frances.

Meanwhile, Roger's woollen trade flourished. In 1575 he had saved sufficient money, in spite of the growing family, to buy Kendal Green House, near Houndhill, together with five fields adjacent. These lands had once been part of the property of Monk Bretton, which was now falling to pieces, assisted by building contractors, to the north-east of the Dale. Roger bought the lands, not directly from the Crown, but from an intermediary called James Crooks,[6] the property was thereafter held of the Crown in soccage, a variety of ancient freehold tenure which did not carry such onerous duties as military service, but which was only subject to agricultural or financial rents. Roger also invested in the purchase of the manor of Silkstone, but in this deal he was partnered by a man called Louis Sawyer, and it has been suggested that the Crown was requested by the freeholders to sell the property. Descendants of these freeholders still claimed to be their own lords of the manor nearly two hundred years later.[7]

Soon after the birth of her tenth child, Mary, and almost certainly as a result of that birth, Elizabeth died.[8] Roger remarried[9]: he found a widow brave enough to take both him and his family, now ranging in age from a young man of twenty-one to a new-born infant. The widow, who did not add to the family, was Margaret Jenkinson, née Bentley,[10] widow of a Charles Jenkinson, of Slade Hooton.

It is in this period that the first Elmhirst in uniform appears. National defence in Elizabeth's reign, whether against the Queen of Scots or the King of Spain, was largely based on local armed associations raised by the potentates of the various districts who assumed ranks which bore more relation to the extent of their acres than to their military virtues. A muster of Private Men and Soldiers from the Wapentake of Staincross was held in Barnsley on 4 December 1587, under the command of two local magnates, while the winter storms still kept the Armada in its Tagus shelter.[11] This rally included, from Worsbrough, Roger Elmhirst and Avery Norton, "his man." Roger was a pikeman and paraded "fully furnished" with his instrument, the pike, a fifteen-foot pole topped with a steel head, together with some sort of body armour, breastplate, or antique chainmail, and a helmet of hard leather or steel. Avery Norton, who paraded with Roger, was a token of his master's growing prosperity which

---

[5] Bapt. 3 Feb. 1576/7. Worsbrough Parish Register.
[6] Enrolled Common Pleas. Easter 17, Eliz. P.R.O.
[7] Rev. J. Prince. Hist. of Silkstone. Penistone printed. 1922, p. 7.
[8] Buried or died 30 April 1580 (Wors. Par. Reg.).
[9] Roger Elmhirst's Will, 30 Nov. 1594, gives maiden name of his second wife.
[10] Married 9 June 1582. Wors. Par. Reg.
[11] Hist. Wors., p. 15.

entailed the presence of two potential soldiers. Apart from the evidence of the muster roll, it is known that Roger had a good piece of body armour, together with what he knew as its "furniture" or accoutrements, some seven years later he was bequeathing it to his son.

During the months when England waited for the Spaniard, Roger had other worries more personal. He was involved in a law suit against a Richard Beckett concerning two properties, Dawcroft and Kingswood, which Roger claimed had been held by his ancestors, "for time out of mind", as part of their copyhold lands.[12] In May 1588 the Court of Exchequer ordered an enquiry and depositions were taken at Barnsley in the September following. Roger's first witness said that he knew the two lands in dispute as Banktop and Houndhill, Dawcroft was merely a field attached to one of the properties,[13] he had known Roger for forty-three years and that the Elmhirsts had been copyholders and had done the appropriate duties and services for them all the time that he could recollect; he had heard that this was also true of the period prior to the dissolution of Nun Appleton.[14] An old man of eighty was another witness who actually remembered that the two properties were indeed copyhold before the dissolution of Nun Appleton. The remainder of this dispute has not survived among the Exchequer records: it is certain that Roger and his friends were absolutely correct in all their statements: it is also certain that Roger won the case.[15]

Roger's second wife, the ex-widow Margaret, died on 22 November 1593. But this time Roger, now a widower for the second time, was not so troubled with young children. Mary, his youngest daughter, was already thirteen and the eldest were married with families of their own.

On 30 November 1594, Roger, who called himself a yeoman, a dying man, made his will. He asked to be buried with his ancestors and left various small sums to the poor of Worsbrough, Barnsley and Stainbrough. To his eldest son he left his corslet and its accoutrements, with which he had doubtless paraded seven years before; Silkstone and the lands at Kendal Green, leased out at the time, also went to his eldest son[16] on condition that various younger sons and daughters were paid £5 each. The eldest son was also made responsible for the schooling of the two youngest children. Elizabeth, the eldest daughter, was left the best silver spoon; each of the grandchildren got a ewe lamb of their own. God-children and servants at Houndhill each had a shilling. John, the second son, received some property in Stainborough, "which I have of the demise

---

[12] P.R.O. Exchequer Proceedings.
[13] This is as true to-day as it was in 1536. Dawcroft, divided into Upper and Nether Dawcroft, is land lying to the south of Elmhirst to which it belongs.
[14] Evidence of Wm. Micklethwaite.
[15] Evidence of Wm. Walker and others. Exchequer Depositions, P.R.O., E.134, 9 and 10 Chas. I. Hillary 11, 7 Jan. 1633.
[16] Yet it is his younger son Roger "of London, gentleman", who, together with Louis Sawyer, leased the land in 1607 to Swift and Greaves of Silkstone, letting also the iron mills and giving authority to work and dig ironstone and coal. (Rev. Joseph Prince. *Hist. of Silkstone*. Penistone printed. 1922, p. 97.)

of Henry Everingham'', and the apparatus for cloth production, two looms, tenter shears, a dyeing lead and £20. This John, now aged thirty, was apparently employed by another Everingham, Francis of Stainbrough,[17] because Francis was left a filly foal "desiring him to be a good master to my son John." Remaining children got £26 13s. 4d. each.

This was the will of a substantial yeoman. There is an interesting omission, the flocks, except for lambs, one each for the grand-children, are not mentioned. Possibly Roger had already given these to his eldest son. Houndhill, being copyhold, was not mentioned: Elmhirst would also not be officially his to bequeath.

The day after making his will, old Roger died.

---

[17] Stainborough passed to the Everinghams by marriage in the reign of Henry III and was sold to the Cutlers in 1602.

GENERATION VIII

ROBERT ELMHIRST OF HOUNDHILL AND ELMHIRST
1559-1618

The man who succeeded his father in 1594 and who inherited a considerable fortune for a north country yeoman, was apparently a hopeless muddler, however, for a few years at least, things went deceptively well under the impetus that they had gained from his enterprising father.

Robert, when he came into the property, was thirty-five and probably still unmarried. Single, too, was his second brother John, now thirty, who had inherited the apparatus for manufacturing cloth. William and Roger, the younger brothers, were twenty-two and eighteen respectively. His sister, Elizabeth had married Robert Castleford,[1] a prosperous widower. Margaret, a younger sister, married Roger Genn of Ouslethwaite.[2]

Robert Elmhirst must have wedded shortly after succeeding his father: 1596 is the most likely date. Though his wife was only about twenty-five years old, she was already a widow, her late husband, Mark Foxcroft, had left her a certain amount of household and other property; her maiden name had been Elizabeth Thornton, her father William Thornton of Thornton. Socially she was superior to the yeoman Elmhirsts; through her mother half her blood was that of the great house of Tempest, that had honoured itself at Agincourt and, more recently, perhaps not quite so honourably, had captured Henry VI after the Battle of Towton. From the Tempests in their turn through the Hollands and the Le Zouches, she had both Alfred and Charlemagne among her ancestors. Through her father she was descended from lines of Vavasours, Gascoignes and Mowbrays.

Richard, their eldest son, was probably born in 1597, and other children followed rapidly.[3] To the old stone building at Houndhill it became necessary to build or replace a second wing, which still stands, the dark timbering with "R.E. 1606" on the gable, contrasting strongly with the light stone that composes the older wing, stone most probably acquired at a cheap rate when the contractors clawed like vultures at the dead whale of great Bretton Priory, tearing the fabric off, leaving naked arches, the fleshless ribs, all that was left of the once mighty living creature.[4]

---

[1] 14 Dec. 1585. Wors. Par. Reg.
[2] 29 Sept. 1603. Wors. Par. Reg.
[3] Elizabeth bapt., 1 Sept. 1600; Robert, 5 Sept. 1602; Sarah, 5 Aug. 1604; William, 20 July 1606; and Judith, 14 March 1609-1610. (Wors. Par. Reg.)
[4] In 1567 the Everinghams were buying "ornamental stonework" from the Priory ruins. *Stainbrough and Rockley.* 1853, p. 8.

Robert and his brother John[5] continued with their father's cloth manu-facturing: as their younger brothers became old enough they, too, assisted in retailing the material both locally and in London, where young Roger seems to have acted as a sort of commercial traveller.

Meanwhile, the ordinary business of farming in Worsbroughdale went on as it had always done: a few of the manorial records of between the years 1605 and 1608 have survived.[6] At this time the Crown still owned the manor, otherwise the listed details of offences and penalties could have been taken word for word from mediaeval records. In April 1605 there were fines for ploughing up the baulks of land which separated properties. A year later thirty-two swine were wandering about the manor; Robert owned one and had to pay four pence. Next spring, 1607, he had five pigs wandering and had to pay two pence for each animal; in 1608 a roaming pig of Robert's appeared again.[7]

The last of these manor rolls shows that then, October 1608, Robert Castleford had just died and his son William was paying his fine on taking over his father's copyhold lands. This meant that Robert Elmhirst's sister, Elizabeth, was now a widow. After her bereavement she relied more and more on Robert's advice in the management of the properties, which included Darley Cliffe,[8] that had been left her. She married next a gentleman called John Booth, grown old and wealthy in the service of the famous Earl of Shrewsbury.

Robert was now free to concentrate on his own financial ruin: perhaps the sheep became infected with some epidemic: perhaps woollen cloth went out of fashion: perhaps there were newer and better ways of weaving or dyeing cloth: perhaps his brothers lacked that combination of garrulousness and self-esteem that marks the born salesman. Whatever the reason, business dwindled as debts and obligations grew.

Before the final crash came, Robert did have a small success. Knowing that his new brother-in-law, John Booth, was rich, he went over to meet him at Rotherham and talked him into considering the purchase of the manor of Worsbrough from the Crown, which had held it since the dissolution. The Crown needed money desperately and was selling its lands cheaply. Booth knew little or nothing about Worsbroughdale, but in any case was not averse to having his money well invested in those days of clipped coinage and arbitrary fines.

Evidence by one of Booth's servants still remains; he related how he was called into the house at Hansworth Woodhouse, where Booth and Robert were in conference. Booth told him to saddle up for a long journey to carry

---

[5] Married Elizabeth Oxley, 24 Oct. 1597. Wors. Par. Reg.
[6] Worsbrough Court Rolls. P.R.O. S.C.2. 211. 159.
[7] P.R.O. S.C.2: 211.159.
[8] Hist. Wors., p. 177.

a letter to Mr. William Elmhirst, Robert's brother and agent, at his house in the City of London. When he got there the servant handed the letter to William, who opened it in his presence, read some of it and "thereupon in a passion cast the said letter aside on a table, and said in the presence and hearing of this deponent: 'Doth my brother Robert think that I have nothing else to do with my money but to buy land for him. I have already disbursed my money for land in Ireland.' Yet afterwards, when William Elmhirst had read right through the letter, he promised to do his best for the said John Booth and Robert Elmhirst, for the obtaining of the purchase of the manor on their behalf, and sent a letter back by this deponent."[9]

Robert and his two youngest brothers avoided great financial outlay but certainly "took great pains in the buying of the manor for John Booth."[10] Booth, in his turn, was grateful to Robert for all his trouble and thereafter agreed to lower the rent on the Elmhirst copyhold lands in what was now his manor from nineteen shillings and ten pence a year to only two shillings. At the same time, Robert made certain that no more than this would in future be paid by subsequent Elmhirsts who came into the properties. This change of rent was later to be the cause of considerable argument and lawsuits. Fortunately for Robert and his successors, old Booth ordered his manor steward to confirm this alteration in writing and inserted the change also in his will; moreover he lived long enough after making his will to accept the first year's rent at the new rate.[11] Booth asked others attending his Manor Court what they thought about Elmhirst's new rent. They "answered they were pleased with it, " adding cautiously, "so that he laid not the burden upon others within the said manor."[12]

Robert's opponents later said that he had wheedled these concessions out of his senile brother-in-law and that he had also persuaded him to make the entry in the will. It was even to be alleged that Robert had made the entry in the will in "a remote roome from him [John Booth], others excluded."[13] This accusation was easily disproved by the clerk, who actually wrote the will; far from dictating or altering it privately, Robert Elmhirst was not even in the house at the time.

Old John Booth died[14] soon after buying the manor, leaving a daughter, Elizabeth, as his heiress; she married first a Castleford, who only survived his father-in-law for a year, and then, secondly, Gervase Hanson. The connections were intricate but important; so many married so often. Robert Castleford married twice (his second wife being Elizabeth Elmhirst). John Booth married

[9] Exchequer Depositions. Barnsley, 7 Jan. 1633. Evidence of John Nodder.
[10] *Richard Elmhirst v. The Hansons.* P.R.O. C.21. E. 19.8.
[11] *Richard Elmhirst v. The Hansons.* P.R.O. C.21. E 19.8. Evidence of Francis West. 8 April 1624.
[12] *Richard Elmhirst v. The Hansons.* P.R.O. C 21. E 19.8. Evidence of Richard Micklethwaite [1616].
[13] *Richard Elmhirst v. The Hansons.* P.R.O. C 21. E 19.8. 1626.
[14] In 1613.

twice (his second wife being the same Elizabeth Elmhirst, now Widow Castle-ford), and John Booth's daughter married twice, first to William the son of Robert Castleford, and secondly to this Gervase Hanson.

The year of this single stroke of good business, the lowering of the copyhold rent, was, it seems, the year of financial collapse. The partnership of the Elmhirst brothers was broken. John, the second brother, lived thereafter in Lewdine, in Worsbrough.[15] The two youngest, William and Roger, for some undiscoverable reason, entered the Customs. In these times Customs' posts were all farmed out; perhaps the brothers invested the remains of their money in the purchase of posts. William, who had spent his money on lands in Ireland, had had his Customs' position for a considerable period, being sometimes described as Haberdasher and sometimes as "of the Custom House". His wife Susan had seen their children die,[16] only a daughter, Margaret, is recorded as having grown up.[17] This William, himself a veteran of the Law Courts,[18] reached obscurity in Ireland, where he was still living in 1634, unkindly described as a "decayed Chapman" by those who had no reason to like him.[19]

Roger, a slightly less decayed Chapman, also left England about the year 1613 and reappears, the Irish Sea between him and his business world, a Customer in the wild port of Limerick; he died soon after.[20]

Unfortunate Robert, burdened with a growing family, had no such easy route of escape. Gervase Hanson, who had some employment in the Notaries Office in the Court of Common Pleas, agreed to act as his solicitor and together they fought a number of rearguard actions against a horde of creditors. London became unhealthy for Robert: he was arrested for debt and was, as his widow later admitted, "ready to be cast into the Counter upon that arrest" if Hanson had not arranged bail. Never again after this escape did he venture back to London.[21]

These lawsuits make rather depressing reading even after the lapse of centuries. One or two will serve as examples.

Francis Ainsworth, Citizen and Draper of London, had had dealings with the Elmhirst brothers in London for many years and ''resting fully resolved of the honesty and good dealings of the said Robert and Roger Elmhirst, was not soe carefull as he might have been in demandinge any acquittance or notes

---

[15] In 1615 he found a second wife, Dorothy Allott. Wors. Par. Reg.
[16] 26 March 1602. Buried, "Ellen Elmhurst, daughter of William Elmhurst, Haberdasher, a yeare old, her pit by Jane Buttler's in ye church." 30 April 1603. Buried, "William Elmhurst an infant of William Elmhurst 20 weekes old." (Both in St. Peter's, Cornhill, Register.)
[17] Marriage Licence, Jan. 1638, to John Harrison. Mar. Lic. Alleg. London, Book 20, p. 35.
[18] *John Bullock* v. *William E.*, in Chancery. P.R.O. B. 28.5. (1620.)
[19] Exchequer Deposition, 1634.
[20] Evidence of Eliz. Booth. Exchequer Depositions, P.R.O., E 134.9 and 10, Chas. I, Hil. II. 17 Jan. 1634.
[21] *Richard E.* v. *The Hansons.* Evidence of Eliz. Elmhirst and Thos. Hanson, 1626. P.R.O., C 21. E 19.8.

under their handwrightinge" for various debts paid to them. Then, he said, Robert "having some spleane, & having conceived some causeless displeasure against him", claimed non-payment of debts for which he had never bothered to obtain the receipts. So Ainsworth optimistically asked for protection.[22]

Robert answered that the debts were never settled and he was still owed "for divers and several parcels of clothes". He alleged that Ainsworth had threatened him, saying he was prepared to make a long lawsuit of the business so that it would cost Robert much more than the £10 he claimed by the time all the lawyers had been paid.[23] He said, too, that Ainsworth had been as good as his word, had taken the suit to the Court of King's Bench and by Chancery subpoena had already compelled him to make an unnecessary and expensive journey of 130 miles from Yorkshire to the London Law Courts.[24]

Then there was a bigger case against a man called Peace. A woollen chapman, Robinson of Wakefield, had gone bankrupt; Robert, among others, had settled some of Robinson's debts and claimed his London stock-in-trade as compensation. This stock was temporarily left in the charge of the bankrupt's own apprentice named Peace, who was told by the creditors to sell it. Peace, however, had disposed of only some of it; had, it was alleged, conspired with the bankrupt Robinson and kept no accounts at all. Peace said that £600, which Robert told him to pay to a City Alderman called Askwith, had indeed been forthcoming out of the proceeds of the sale; but the Alderman, who should have known, said the money had never reached him and he was, in consequence, sueing Robert. Robert complained, in addition, of other dishonest dealings by Peace, who owed him money for small amounts of "Northern cloth".[25]

In his defence, Peace said that he knew Robert stood bound for his former master Robinson, but because of his own position as an apprentice, he naturally knew no details. Moreover, he was never left in charge of all the property and so could not account for what had happened. As regards the alderman's £600, this witness thought it had been paid; he had heard his master say so. Regarding all the small complaints that Robert made, he would only admit a debt of six shillings for a rug; this he was willing to pay at any time.[26]

Even back in the comparative seclusion of Houndhill, Robert seemed to collect acuter troubles to add to the perpetual debts. In 1615 another lawsuit threatened; this time over the felling of a tree, something significant but absurdly trivial to a man in as much trouble as Robert. It was, however, settled by arbitration.[27]

---

[22] *Francis Ainsworth* v. *Robert Elmhirst*. 19 Oct. 1614. P.R.O., C 2. A 7.54.
[23] *Ibid.* 24 Nov. 1614.
[24] The end of this lawsuit is not discoverable. There is no Chancery decision recorded in either 1614 or 1615.
[25] *Robert Elmhirst* v. *Robinson & Peace*. 28 July 1615. P.R.O. C2. E7.14.
[26] *Robert Elmhirst* v. *Robinson & Peace*. 5 July 1615. P.R.O. C.2. E.7.14.
[27] *Richard Elmhirst* v. *The Hansons*. Evidence of Robert Rockley, 1626. P.R.O. C 21. E 19.8.

In 1616 and 1617 Robert stayed quietly at home in Houndhill, but even here he was not safe: he dug for coal[28] and again used the timber from his copyhold lands.[29] Jealous eyes were watching him. In many manors coal belonged indisputedly to the lord and while a copyholder was usually entitled to use wood to keep his premises in repair or for fuel, they were often not permitted to cut it for sale. However, Hanson, now Lord of the Manor, was related by marriage and though Robert's actions were noted, only the tree-felling, the trees were ashes, was reported in the manor courts. Robert answered that he had "deeds or charters to warrant the same", which he never subsequently produced. As will appear later, the whole business was not as futile as it seems. Robert was claiming his copyhold lands were his to do with practically as he liked, though he admitted certain of the copyhold restrictions. The Hansons, on the other hand, wanted absolute control themselves, claiming that copyholders were nothing more than former serfs with rights to nothing, enjoying gracious privileges. Robert, according to a certain witness's memory, was once heard to admit that his ancestors were serfs, but that they had been granted their freedom. A significant observation if made indeed[30].

It was in this gloomy atmosphere of debts and lawsuits that he made his will. He arranged that all the profits from his copyhold lands for four years should go towards the payment of his debts. Then, realising that his debts had not diminished, he lengthened the period to six years. He died in the spring of 1618 and was buried with his ancestors.[31]

---

[28] *Ibid.* Evidence of Roger Genn, 1626. P.R.O. C 21. E 19.8.
[29] *Ibid.* Evidence of Thos. Hanson.
[30] Exchequer Interrogation. Barnsley, 7 Jan. 1633. P.R.O. E 134. 9 & 10 Chas. I, Hil. II. Hugh Everett, Clerk, stated that he had "heard the sd. Robt. (as he thinketh) say that some of his ancestors were manumised touching the said bondage."
[31] Buried 9 April 1618 (Wors. Par. Reg.).

GENERATION IX

RICHARD ELMHIRST OF HOUNDHILL AND ELMHIRST
[1597]-1654

When badgered Robert died on 9 April 1618, his eldest son Richard was not yet of age. Parish records being in this period imperfectly kept, the date of his birth cannot be accurately ascertained. However, Richard was accepted as having reached his majority within a few months. It seems likely that he was studying law at this time, again there is no record of this, but the family tradition is made more probable by the fact that in after life Richard seemed to know very well the law and all its intricacies. Perhaps he had seen how legal ignorance had something to do with the downfall of his father.

His mother, the widowed Elizabeth, was thrown into understandable despair when the full details of her late husband's debts came to light. She had been named as executrix in his will by which six years' income from the copyhold lands was to go towards the appeasement of creditors. Wisely she refused to undertake this duty that had been laid upon her; in her panic she went straight to Gervase Hanson, told him she was going to renounce the executrixship and "refuse to meddle with her husband's goods" and at the same time made "great moan and lamentation [before him] touching her troubles and crosses and for that her husband's debts amounted to much more than she expected." Hanson said that he thereupon tried to comfort her and promised that he would not himself press for payment until all the other creditors had been satisfied.

As a first instalment of the payment of the debts, the administrators made an inventory of her husband's goods, incidentally including some of her own property left her by her first husband, and these things were sold.[1]

More clouds darkened the horizon. At the next meeting of the manor court the widow was admitted to the copyhold estates, a third of it as her own dower and two-thirds to hold during Richard's minority. Even at this time old Elizabeth seems to have suspected that all was not well: she told the steward that she wished to take no more than a third of her husband's holdings, leaving the remainder for her son. Her protests, though heard by others then present, were overruled; she was told to take it all or leave it all, and so, still protesting, she was admitted to the entire property. By this admission, as she had probably been warned by friends, she was going back to the old mediaeval custom by which serfs' widows came into all their husbands' holdings. In Worsbrough this method had only been revived in recent years, in the recent past when the manor had been held by the Crown, widows had been admitted to only third part.[2]

---

[1] Evidence, Elizabeth Elmhirst, *Richard Elmhirst* v. *The Hansons*. P.R.O. C 21. E. 19.8.
[2] At the end of legal disputes Elizabeth did keep a third part only. *Royalist Composition Papers*. Y.A.S. Records, vol. XV, p. 347.

When, a month or two later, Richard came of age, his appearance at the court to claim his copyhold lands was commanded on three consecutive occasions. He never appeared. His reason for this is hard to understand, possibly he hoped that by leaving the property in somebody else's nominal charge he thought he could make the land pay better than if all his actions were to be crippled by the terms of his father's will and the watchful administrators. His disobedience in refusing to appear was promptly punished by Hanson as Lord of the Manor, who, by the Manor Court, and quite justifiably, ordered the land to be seized by the court officials.

It seems that Richard, realising he had made a tactical error, later went to a meeting of the manor court and tried unsuccessfully to get himself admitted, even to the extent of offering to pay whatever reasonable fine was inflicted.

By November 1622 feelings were so high that Hanson told one of his court officials to distrain on two of Richard's oxen which were thereupon seized. Richard countered with a legal injunction compelling the official to appear in York to answer for his actions, either to show cause or to return the oxen; when he got there, he found that no charge had been made out against him.[3]

Until this moment the rent reductions fixed by dead John Booth had not been challenged. Now, however, in 1623, Hanson refused to accept the small sum of two shillings and asked why it had been lowered from the nineteen shillings and tenpence. He even went so far as to suggest that if old Booth had indeed reduced the rent for Richard's father, then Booth must have been persuaded against his will when he was too senile to realise what he was doing. Hanson put himself very much in the wrong in this case; not only had Booth accepted the two shillings from Richard's father, but the manor court officials, and these men had recently represented Hanson, had always accepted it. Moreover, as has been seen, Booth had recorded the change not only by legal deed but also in his will.

Next year it was Richard's turn to act as Court greave at the meetings of the Manor Court. Because of all the disputes and thinking perhaps that if he accepted this duty he would be harried unnecessarily, or perhaps not wishing to be demonstrably in an inferior position to the Lord of the Manor, he refused to do his duty. Hanson was forced therefore to fill the place with a substitute, who was paid thirty shillings for doing what Richard should have done for nothing. Young Richard then baited his deputy with "malicious acts" so that the hireling was "pestered and encumbered with justices' warrants" and bound to appear at the Sessions, where nothing was objected against him (the successful York manoeuvre repeated).

Hanson found his grievances accumulating, he remembered all the debts still owing by dead Robert's heirs, the multitude of cases where he had acted

---

[3] Evidence, Nicholas Medley. *Richard Elmhirst* v. *The Hansons.* P.R.O. C 21. E 19.8.

as legal adviser to Robert, even the debt owing to Hanson himself had never been paid. He brooded on how Richard was making free of his copyhold estates by selling the timber and digging for coal; he thought, moreover, of his persecuted hireling court greave.

Richard on his side had his grievances, his inheritance had been a battle-ground, his mother forced into a sinister copyholding position, his oxen seized and his every movement on what seemed his own lands watched and made the subject of complaint. It was he who started the long drawn case in Chancery that was to last two years and more. Such Chancery cases were largely a matter of question and answer; both plaintiff and defendant compiled a questionnaire to be administered to the witnesses they could muster. From the replies and by a process of cross-question, the truth had to be reached. In his first list of questions Richard tried to show that the rent had indeed been legally reduced to two shillings. Then he got witnesses to agree with him that copyholders could both cut trees and dig for coal without interference. Lastly, he proved that widows should only be admitted to a third of their husband's estates and that his mother had been unwillingly compelled to accept all her late husband's copyhold lands.

The first series of answers to Richard's questionnaire is dated 8 April 1624; the second, 14 April 1626, was held in Worsbrough by the commission from the Court of Chancery.

Gervase Hanson's interrogatory was originally a simple document designed to prove that Booth had only bought the property after great sacrifices by his daughter, now Hanson's wife, and that the manor custom was that the widows of "Copyholders or bond Tenants" should be admitted to all their husband's lands. Hanson went on to demonstrate to his own satisfaction that Richard and all his Elmhirst ancestors were of servile origin and therefore held their copyhold lands as did any other manor serfs. Not only was a serf's widow admitted to all her late husband's holdings, but, copyholders being unfree, they were expressly forbidden, without the lord's permission, to treat either the timber or the soil as their own.

To prove these points Hanson and his steward studied the manor records to find evidence the source of which is now lost, together with the Court Rolls. Such evidence, because it is partisan, must be suspect. On the other hand, the Chancery Commission would and could easily detect any false statement, and there is no reason to suppose that Hanson's witnesses were perjured.

The nature of the evidence can be gained entirely from the questions: the witnesses, Thomas Oke of Thurgoland and Thomas Hanson, the defendant's brother, both add nothing new by their affirmative answers. Since this information refers to mediaeval times, it is here transcribed in full :

"Question 6.—Does it also appear in the same Court Rolls and other evidence that the Ancestors of the Complainant's father and others that [have] Copyhold land there have been entitled and styled 'Nativi tenentes or tenentes in bondagio' or termed 'held and in bondage'?[4]

"And whether doth it thereby also appear that the complainant's ancestors or generation or some of them have been reputed, used or esteemed as villeins or bondmen of that Manor or presented or fined for putting their children to school without licence of the Lady Prioress of Nun Appleton then owner of the said Manor?

"Question 7.—Does it also appear in the Rolls that a presentment was made by the suitors or homagers in Anno 4to. Henr. 4 [1402-1403] that one William the son of William Elmhirst the Lord's villein was fled or escaped forth of the said Manor of Worsbrough. And whether was a precept thereupon recorded to be awarded to the Court guard there to take or apprehend him and bring him to his judgement?

"Question 8.—Does it also appear that these called bond tenants and now called copyhold tenants were often presented or punished for waste, spoil or decay of their copyholds or the woods or trees thereupon growing. Or for using or disposing thereof upon any freehold land. And whether doth it also appear that such tenants have compounded to pay a yearly rent for breaking the soil and getting coals?"

When all this was still going on, debts owing, cattle impounded and court-greave baiting, Richard caused a summons to be made out against the Hansons for them to appear at Doncaster Sessions. Records are imperfect concerning this incident and the parchments are largely illegible: it was probably in August 1625. On Michaelmas fair day at Barnsley, and on an allegedly trifling matter, he even had Hanson's wife kept in custody for a while.

After this insult Hanson added more questions to his interrogatory concerning this "greater charge and vexation" and then tried to prove that Richard might have been admitted to his father's copyhold lands "if his father's will had been performed and the profits of the land disposed according to the surrender and will reported to be made for that purpose."[5] Hanson also found his brother willing to witness that from ancient manor documents he:

"is persuaded in his conscience that the lands now claimed by the plaintiff were anciently the land of the Marryets before the same came to the plaintiff's ancestors, because that the lands of the Marryetts and the lands of Elmhirst were both of like number of messuages, oxgangs and rents to the lord and that when the names of the Mariots ceased to be mentioned in the later Rolls, which were in the more ancienter, there were put in those later Rolls the name of Elmhirst."

This very intriguing suggestion of Thomas Hanson's can obviously be no more value than as a guess—only one piece of contemporary evidence remains.[6]

---

[4] A contemporary authority supports this view of the Hansons. Fitzherbert says that "copyhold is but a new term, in the old times they were called tenants in villeinage or base tenure". Chas. Calthorpe. *The Relation of the Lord of the Manor and the Copyholder*. London, 1635. This cannot affect the certainty that freemen could become copyholders and not thereby lose their freedom.

[5] Evidence of Thos. Hanson. *Richard Elmhirst v. The Hansons*. P.R.O. C 21. E 19.8.

[6] The Poll Tax of the 6th year of Edward III (1332) is still extant in the Public Record Office (E. 179. 206/15). Thirteen men were then taxed in Worsbrough and among them is no Elmhirst but one Robert Mariote. There is no Robert among those who had not then acquired surnames: it remains possible that the Robert Mariote who does not appear after 1332 may well be identical with the Robert of Elmhirst who is unrecorded before 1340.

Gervase Hanson then made out a third series of questions, more irrelevant and more offensive. He seems to have been forced to admit that John Booth had indeed lowered the Elmhirsts' rent and had recorded this change in his will. But now Hanson attacked the genuineness of the will. "Did not Robert Elmhirst direct, advise or dictate the same? Was the bequest [of a lowered rent] to Robert Elmhirst written in the testator's presence or in a remote room from him, whether were others excluded by Robert Elmhirst when the same was doing?" Then he asked his witnesses more about the ancient manor customs "fifty years or more before the suppression of the Abbey", regarding both the widow's inheritance, the cutting of timber and the digging of coal. Looking for more mud to throw, he found it easily in the slough of debts left by poor dead Robert, for whom Hanson had acted as solicitor, and in the very presence of Richard's old uncle, John, who had just died,[7] but who had been living at Dawcroft without, it was claimed, any right at all since he had never had the permission of the Lord of the Manor.

Then all Robert's lawsuits were paraded again. "Do you know that the defendant as attorney or solicitor for Robert Elmhirst did present suit at law or in Chancery, or obtained any judgement for Robert Elmhirst against Harman, Carpenter, Chapman, Culton, Fullers, Francis Beesley, Randal Fenton, Robert Ashmore, one Kitchinman and other inhabitants about Aldwark? Or Roger Cawood, servant to Robert Elmhirst, against Henry Walker, Nicholas Walker, John Wright, William Allen, John Randle alias Chadwick? Or for Robert Elmhirst himself against the said Walker and against Richard Wood, one Mabb, one Baxter Clayton and his wife, one Fells a serjeant, one Robinson, one Jopson Brooke, alderman Middleton, or against any of them?"

Because of all these law suits Hanson then claimed that Robert's heirs still owed him legal fees and other costs. Then, he said "the defendant, because of the many weighty and tedious suits and causes he had entered into for Robert Elmhirst, withdrew or less used or practised his employment of clerkship in the chief notary's office of the Common Pleas", and "would not such a clerkship have brought him, if continued, more lawful profit and clear recompense than his following or soliciting country suits?"

Lastly, because by now arrangements by the Hansons to sell the manor to Sir Francis Wortley had been completed, was not Hanson being practically forced out of his property by the "uttermost malice" and persistent persecution from Richard Elmhirst?

Hanson did not get all the answers he wanted on these points, his slanderous accusations on the genuineness of Booth's will were unsupported, the hopeless lawsuits of Robert Elmhirst were confirmed in all their multiplicity, he found someone (and probably everyone) to agree that he would have done better to

---

[7] Buried Worsbrough 21 April 1624. (Par. Reg.)

keep his clerkship than get involved in Robert's financial troubles; lastly, a witness was even found who had heard him complain that Richard's persecution had forced him to sell the manor.

Richard's personal reply to all these suggestions still survives in another part of the Record Office.[8] He said that the Hansons themselves knew very well that the Elmhirsts had been freemen for at least two hundred years. The choice of this period is surely of significance since it took one back to 1425 and the latest dated sign of servitude that Hanson had called in evidence was 1409. Alternatively, claimed Richard in his legal style, none of his ancestors had ever been serfs; he brought no counter-evidence on this last claim and there is every reason to suppose he knew, if not at this time, certainly a little later, that it was false. He saw the court entry which recorded the payment of servile merchet and had deliberately ignored that damning sentence. As regards two pieces of property, ten acres to the north of Dawcroft and some land on Darley Cliff, these, said Richard, had never been occupied illegally by his family. He dismissed with ease the myth as to the undue pressure by his father at the time John Booth made his will. He did not deny that he was liable to serve as a Manor Court official, but denied that he was ever requested so to do. Lastly, he argued, if the Hansons claimed that widows took all their husbands' lands, why was he being penalised by being ordered to do the duties of a copyholder himself?

From this prolonged struggle Richard emerged the victor; the rent of two shillings was confirmed and the Hansons quickly left the district. Locally, Richard had proved himself to be a man of some authority; it was during the lawsuit that for the first time an Elmhirst claimed to be a gentleman in the very definite seventeenth century meaning of the word, his opponents, more difficult to convince than Richard himself, studiously avoided the title, calling him Yeoman as his ancestors had been. Never, after Richard's time, was an Elmhirst to be described as yeoman: gentlemen they remained for a century or more till custom promoted them to squiredom.

The year the lawsuit was over Richard's younger brother, then eighteen, entered University College at Oxford[9], where he would have met many whom he knew, at least by sight. Local gentry, three Rockleys and two Wentworths, were at the same college near the same period. Five years after William, another Worsbrough boy, famous and then infamous, Obadiah Walker, was also admitted to University College.

It was during this period that Richard must have been first employed by the great Sir Thomas Wentworth, of Wentworth Woodhouse, a few miles distant.

[8] P.R.O. E 32.104.
[9] He became close friend of the future Sir Geo. Radcliffe, who was to be of such assistance to Richard himself. *Vide* letters from Radcliffe to his mother, 1615-1617 (T. D. Whitaker, *Life and Corres. of Sir Geo. Radcliffe*, 4to. London, 1810).

·Sir Thomas, a couple of years older than Richard, had just succeeded his father as second baronet and was already famous in London. Richard's future was to depend greatly on his service to this rising young man; hopeful descendants once claimed that Richard was his secretary, a portrait of Wentworth with a rabbit-faced scribe was even supposed to show Richard performing his duties.[10] Probably Wentworth had as many secretaries as Wolsey had crossbearers, but the truth seems to be that Richard, famous locally for his knowledge of the law and for his Wentworth-like qualities of industry and determination, was employed in many ways, local and national, as a general agent.

The year that Wentworth was ennobled (1628) Richard found himself a wife,[11] Elizabeth, the daughter of the Richard Micklethwaite, of Swaith Hall in Worsbroughdale, who had appeared "yeoman" in the great lawsuit as a pro-Elmhirst witness.

In 1629 Wentworth was appointed President of the North: as his authority widened so the agent's importance grew and Richard found himself often in York in the wake of the President. What may be one of the earliest introductions of Richard to Wentworth, in his Northern capacity, still survives in the hand of Sir George Radcliffe, that fussy interfering little kinsman of the President's who remained loyal to his master before and after his execution, and who was to partner Richard in many of his later transactions: "May it please your Lordship,—I have appointed Rich. Elmhirst to attend yr. Lop's. tyme, when you shall be pleased to command his service and he will dispatch his owne occasions at home in the meanwhile."[12] Radcliffe called William Elmhirst (Richard's brother) "cousin"[13] when they were at University College together; similarly Wentworth used to call Radcliffe "cousin" until familiarity made him "dear George" at the end of the tyrant's life.[14]

By 1630 Richard had bought himself some property in York for £250,[15] a house and two cottages in Lendall.[16] For a few more years he spent a great deal of his time there, a minor figure on the fringe of the despotic Northern Council, an efficient satellite reflecting the harder brilliance of the Northern Sun. This life of Richard's came to an end in 1632 when King Charles transferred Wentworth to Ireland as his Lieutenant-General, there to be thorough in the digging of their common grave. Richard had other and more personal reasons for leaving York; his young wife had just died and was buried there at St. Helen's Church.[17]

---

[10] The lesser figure in this picture, which is at Blenheim, is now known to be Sir Philip Mainwaring. Even in Worsbroughdale another man, Edmunds, was known to his descendants as Wentworth's secretary.
[11] Married 6 Jan. 1628. Wors. Par. Reg.
[12] Written from York, 31 July 1629. (Wentworth Woodhouse MSS., Sheffield Library.)
[13] T. D. Whitaker, *Life and Corres. of Sir Geo. Radcliffe.* London, 1810.
[14] Revd. W. Knowler, *The E. of Strafford's Letters, etc.* Dublin, 1740.
[15] Notes at end of Pedigree Roll. 1638.
[16] Yorks. Arch. Soc. Records, vol. XV, p. 348, 1893.
[17] Buried 2 Oct. 1632 in the choir of St. Helen's.

Over her grave he caused to be inscribed a most beautiful epitaph,[18] now perished, as if to show that hard heads and soft hearts are not necessarily strangers[19]:

MARGARET ELMHIRST

Thus the earth, broken up by Fate,

Returns to the earth

And one tiny shining star is hidden.

Behold how gems

Polished and cut on Earth,

And small fallen stars, destined to return,

Make up the Heavens.

Back to Houndhill Richard brought two motherless children: Elizabeth, the first-born; Thomas, his only son and heir. Three weeks after his wife had died in York his little boy was buried in Worsbrough. Again Richard sought comfort in an epitaph, a brass which still survives in the family pew:

This boy no Albian was yet grey hair'd borne,

Who saw olde age and night as soon as morne,

His grave a cradle, there his God him lay'd,

Betimes to sleep, lest he the wanton played.

Bid him good night i' th' bed of dust sleep on

Until the morne of Resurrection.

---

[18] J. B. Morell: *Biography of a Common Man in the City of York.* Batsford, 1947. The original Latin version will be found in Drake's *Eboracum*, 1736.

[19] During this same year Richard was involved in another lawsuit, a complicated affair dealing with non-payment of rents, which were owing to him for another small property of his in the city. (*Rich. Elmhirst* v. *Thos. Harrison and Others.* Chancery, 1632. P.R.O. E 4.44.)

By putting three E's in Elmehirste, a sad little anagram was tortured to the shape of "Lo earth misseth me".

He married a second wife, Elizabeth, daughter of John Waite, of Haxby, near York.[20] Now that Wentworth never came to Wentworth Woodhouse, there were probably duties on that estate as well as on his own. Moreover affairs of the Northern Council still occupied his time, Wentworth in Ireland got regular letters from his personal secretary, one of which describes an odd financial manoeuvre[21] and another its possible sequel:

> "I feare you remember not divers great somes of moneye wch. I have payd in the Contrye, wch. I could not have donne without the helpe of those moneys wch. Your honor is informed lyes still at York: I have [borrowed] of Mr. Elmehirste parte of recusants' rents, wch. I must make good in that account out of your Lps. rents, the some of £900."[22]

> "Mr. Elmhirste is gone to London sent for in great haist to showe his book of recaits: what my Lord Treasurer intends by his curiossity I cannot imagine, but I am sure he can find nothing in my hand."[23]

Richard was buying land shrewdly in the neighbourhood of Houndhill. Already, between 1630 and 1637, he had acquired two properties of which the first and biggest was Heeley, a large place of some 250 acres with a rent-roll of £75 a year[24]; to buy it he raised £1,000, helped by his new father-in-law.[25] The second purchase, Genn Farm, lying next to Ouselthwaite, was a piece of the Manor of Worsbrough.

In addition he was busy with a fresh lawsuit. His brother, William, late of University College and now of Wadham, seems to have asked him to invest some of his money for him. Or else Richard was buying property in his brother's name for some subtler reason; his enemies said that it was because William, being in Oxford, could not be so conveniently brought to justice. Whatever the reason, Richard, nominally acting for his brother, claimed to have bought a property in the dale unpleasantly known as the Glewhouse (which has been since transmuted to the View House and refined to The Yews). Richard subsequently had difficulty in collecting the rents, two of the tenants thought it ought to be paid to somebody else. He went personally to demand the money, in the first case threatening "to make the lease nought" and then, being lawyer-trained, compelling his first victim, now thoroughly cowed, to accompany him "so that he could witness him take possession of the Glewhouse in the name of . . . William Elmhirst." Richard had tried to do this before, but on that

---

[20] Paver's Marriage Licences, 1633.

[21] Wentworth's juggling with his personal accounts and those of the Recusants' Fines continued for many more years: "in Truth the chief Benefit of the Place," as he said when he sent later instructions for Richard. (Revd. W. Knowler. *The Earl of Strafford's Letters*, II, p. 123. Dublin, 1740. [The Lord Deputy to Mr. Rockley, 20 Oct. 1637].)

[22] Rich. Marris to Wentworth. 14 Oct. 1633. Wentworth Woodhouse MSS., Sheffield Library.

[23] Rich. Marris to Wentworth, 10 Feb. 1634. Wentworth Woodhouse MSS., Sheffield Library.

[24] Richard's private "Survey," 1638.

[25] Richard's "Instructions," 1638.

occasion his approach had been the reverse of stealthy and the tenants, slamming the doors, had refused to admit him. This time he was more successful; later the widow who occupied the house alleged that it was Richard's ceaseless persecution of her late husband which had hustled him into an untimely grave "with overmuch grief and terror."[26] Undeterred by such temporary setbacks, Richard's dealings in real estate went on; about the year 1635,[27] he bought two farms in Kirkby Knowle for £200 and another in Altringham for £84. He sold both soon after and acquired a larger property at Higham, a mile and a half to the north-west of Houndhill, which cost him £340 for the 45 acres,[28] but which brought a return of £20 a year.[29] This last property at Higham was claimed by the Wentworths as being part of their manor of Barugh, but as Richard later wrote: "Sir Tho. Wentworth brought a Triall against Richard Elmhirste for the pretended service but durst not try it."[30] Next year marked the last of his larger acquisitions: he bought territory this time at South Ottrington, which he re-sold about a twelvemonth later and about the same time he added some 26 acres in five fields (Oxclose, Jowet Royd, Osmondcroft, Dyke Ing and Hilly Close) to the ancient heritage of Elmhirst.

He had become a rich man. He sat down at Christmastime in 1638 to describe his properties; that same month his second wife had given birth to a son, to be baptised Richard on the first day of January 1639-1640.[31] Only twenty years before he had come into the copyhold estates where his unhappy father had been hiding from his creditors: within that score of years he had paid as many of his father's debts as he had had to; the lands were now his and unencumbered. He wrote them down field by field, each with its area to the nearest quarter of a perch. Ancestral Houndhill was 73 acres, Elmhirst was newly swollen to 70 acres, grandfather Roger's purchase of Kendal Green Farm added another 15 acres to this central core of land in Worsbrough. Now he had added 253 acres of Heeley and the 45 of Higham. Underneath the columns of figures he wrote:

> "Soe I have in the West ridinge four hundred three score and four acres twoo Roods twenty nine and three fourths part of a pearch . . . which yealds me now one hundred and fifty four pounds two shillings and foure pence per annum."

There were two deaths in the family. Little nine-year-old Elizabeth, all that was left of his first wife, had joined her brother in the grave. Dead, too, was Richard's only brother William, late of University College, late of Wadham College, and now late vicar of Ledsham, to which he had been appointed under the patronage of Wentworth.[32]

---

[26] Exchequer Depositions. 9 and 10, Chas. I. Hilary II. P.R.O. E.134.
[27] Pedigree Roll of 1638.
[28] Ibid.
[29] Richard's private "Survey," 1638.
[30] Richard's "Instructions," 1638.
[31] Wors. Par. Reg.
[32] Hist. Wors., p. 129.

Richard, proud again in a son, drew up two further important documents. The first he entitled, "Instructions for my Heires touchinge the Title and Tenure of all my lands." In this he gave the details of each of his properties noting every possible claim that could be made against him and how it could be refuted. He traced the history of the properties back, if necessary, to the Middle Ages, noted the succession of the holders and the pertinent deeds in Chancery. The document starts with:

> "Houndhill and Elmhirst are both coppihold and have bene soe devised to my Ancestors for twelve descents last past."

The second document that Richard composed at about the same time is of even more interest since it was the first attempt to compose a coherent pedigree and much of the material which helped in its construction is not now in existence. He started:

> "Our Family as I conceive assumed their surname from a messuage in Worsborough-dale in the County of Yorke, which now ys and for many Ages hath beene, our peculier Inheritance, and doth not appeare by any Evidence that I could ever yet see to have been the inheritance of any other Family. The word Elmehirst signifies a Grove, Holte or Wood of Elmes. There are (as I am credibly informed) diverse Families in Germany of the same Name or very little differing from it but in England noe other that I could ever yet get any Notice of though for my informacon therein I have been very inquisitive."[33]

The documents on which this pedigree was built were chiefly the ancient manor rolls of Worsbrough. These, which Gervase Hanson had quoted in an attempt to prove a servile origin, Richard now searched in a method no less partisan: he must have omitted a great deal not flattering to one self-conscious of new-found gentility. Within seven years the priceless manuscripts to which he referred "remayning in St. Maryes Tower at York" had all been destroyed in the actual flame of civil war. If Richard did not tell the whole truth at least full credit must be given to him for having recorded accurately, there is no evidence of deliberate distortion.

Absent Wentworth, among his other duties as Lord President of the North, had also had the more ignoble title of Receiver of Recusants' Rents. This title he carried with him now that he was Lieutenant-General and Lord Deputy of Ireland. The duty of actually collecting the fines from the unhappy Papists was shared among a few of his more trustworthy assistants; important among them was Richard Elmhirst. In the Calendar of State Papers in the Public Record Office[34] is a printed form, a receipt by Richard Elmhirst, "Deputy Receiver for Co. Lancaster, on behalf of Thomas Viscount Wentworth, Lord

---

[33] He was quite correct in all these statements. There were Elmenhorsts living in Schleswig Holstein at least until the beginning of Hitler's war. Others of the name who flourished in Hamburg used for a coat of arms a silver horseshoe on a field azure. (Rietstap's *L'Armorial Général*.) It is strange but true that none o the places called Elmhurst gave rise to a surname.

[34] *Calendar of State Papers, Domestic*. Chas. I, vol. DXXXVIII. No. 42. Dated 22 Nov. 1638.

Deputy of Ireland, receiver of recusants' rents" (for the sum of £10 paid by Richard Sherburne of Stonyhurst for the recusancy of Elizabeth his wife).[35] For another six years after 1640,[36] he was still keeping his profitable position and had control of the accounts, a point later of great interest to the new rulers of England. It does not seem possible to discover when Richard obtained this unpleasant post of Deputy Collector of Fines levied on those who still professed Roman Catholicism. He certainly held office between 1634 and 1640, because at the end of this period the Vice-President of the Council of the North ordered him to pay, from official funds, certain small amounts towards the costs of various persecutions.[37]

In 1639 Wentworth came back from Ireland, thoroughness and ruthlessness equally demonstrated. He had grown to be Earl of Strafford, chosen by King Charles to chastise Presbyterian Scots with the same iron first he had used against the popish Irish. Richard played a not unimportant part in helping his master get things ready for this punitive expedition against the rebels.

Sir William Uvedale, the Treasurer-at-Wars, wrote to his agent in the north. He said that money for the unpopular Scottish war was slow to come from the surly city of London. Meanwhile the King's forces, collecting in the northern counties, were clamouring for pay; these turbulent troops, mustered around York and Ripon, consisted of three regiments of foot and an unspecified strength of cavalry. The Treasurer promised: "I hope within a few days to send you a considerable sum. Meantime, I would have you, if you have not already paid the £4,000 to Elmhurst, dispose both of that and your £2,000 of the Earl of Northumberland's rents into loans to the regiments."[38] It seems that the military financial crisis was, very temporarily, solved. A fortnight later the Treasurer sent further instructions that unless already given, Richard was not to have the £4,000 "until the army be in better condition".[39] By this correspondence Richard appears as a sort of assistant army paymaster. This role is confirmed by a receipt which was in existence about a century ago,[40] which acknowledges £831 paid by Richard for the maintenance of Danby's regiment for a fortnight.

The conscripted army Strafford led hated him much more than they disliked any Presbyterian: England welcomed the Lowlanders across the border.

To his "Cousin Radcliffe" Wentworth wrote: "Pity me, for never came any man to so lost a business. The army altogether unexercised and unprovided

[35] A woman convert convicted for recusancy could be imprisoned till her husband paid £10 a month or a third of his estate.
[36] Sir George Wentworth succeeded Strafford as Chief Receiver.
[37] Calendar of State Papers, Domestic. Chas. I, vol. DXXXIX, Part I, No. 12. March and April, 1640.
[38] Calendar of State Papers, Domestic. Chas. I, CCCCLXXI, No. 54. 11 Nov. 1640.
[39] Calendar of State Papers, Domestic. Chas. I, CCCCLXXII, No. 24. 24 Nov. 1640.
[40] Transcript by Dr. Richard Elmhirst, circa 1845, among Elmhirst MSS., from Thorne.

of neccessities. Our horse all cowardly, the county from Berwick to York in the power of the Scots, and universal affright in all, a general disaffection to the King's service, none sensible of his dishonour. In one word, here alone to fight with all these evils, without anyone to help. God of his goodness deliver me out of this, the greatest evil of my life.''[41] Faced with this impossible situation, Charles had to call another parliament. This, the Long Parliament of November 1640, met in more determined mood than its short-lived predecessor. Together with the Star Chamber, Parliament now abolished the hated Council of the North and all its arbitrary claims to fine and imprison. Archbishop Laud disappeared into the Tower of London, and Wentworth was swiftly put to death by act of attainder.

The execution of his master and the disappearance of the Council at York made this a most depressing year for Richard, and in the autumn of 1642 the Civil War began.

Apart from his personal sentiments, whatever they may have been, Richard was already committed by his past to the Royalist cause. He had long been the trusted servant of the arch-malignant Wentworth and he was known throughout much of Yorkshire as a former agent of what was declared to have been the criminal Council of the North. Nearly all the local gentry and yeomen, prosperous and unmolested, sided automatically with the King. The King's General, the Earl of Newcastle, had no difficulty in establishing garrisons in neighbouring Barnsley and Doncaster. Rotherham and Sheffield first declared for the Parliament but very shortly after, the Earl of Newcastle approaching, pledged support for the King.[42] In the dale itself the new Lord of the Manor, Edmunds, another of Wentworth's secretaries, declared for the King. Rockley of Rockley in Worsbroughdale, of a line more ancient than any, destined soon to disappear, did the same. Wortley of Wortley, Wentworth of Wentworth, what less could be done by aspiring Elmhirst of Elmhirst?

Richard set about the fortification of his house at Houndhill. Standing as it did on a small hill on a gradual slope, it was at the mercy of any enemy in possession of the higher ridge to the north. Yet from the house itself lay a magnificent view of the lands to the south, over the winding valley of the Dove. To keep it from assault and to double its value as an observation post, Richard intended to ring it with a wall some thirty feet from the house all around. At each bend in the wall there was to be a strong, squat turret well supplied with portholes. Unhappily, only part of the walls with one complete turret, and part of another, remains. Either the enemy came quicker than anticipated, or else when they did come they subsequently made a strenuous and largely successful attempt at demolition.

[41] C. V. Wedgwood, *Strafford*, p. 254. Jonathan Cape, 1938.
[42] Rowland Jackson: *History of Barnsley*, 1858, p. 151.

In the summer of 1643 Sir Thomas Fairfax was in the neighbourhood with an army of the Parliament. Both Rotherham and Wakefield fell to his forces. Apart from these major triumphs, his army would have been continually sending out small companies to smoke amateur malignants from their nests. Thus fell Wortley Hall, fortified at the same time as Houndhill; Wortley himself was imprisoned.[43] Another detachment, or perhaps the same one, came on to Houndhill.

In deciding what happened next, it is difficult to distinguish fact from fiction. None the less so since, for some unknown reason, the Civil War period was so popular with Victorian romanticists of the "When did you last see your father" school. At its most exciting, Fairfax seemed not sure enough of his military capabilities and Oliver Cromwell himself took the responsibility for capturing Houndhill. After a battle in which Richard's garrison of forty soldiers killed at least some of the enemy, the place was overrun. The Roundheads rushed in to seize Richard, thrusting their swords through mattresses, but courteously leaving Richard's wife in her puerperium with a polite: "Good lady be still, we will not harm you." Some parliamentarian shot at Richard, hence the marks on an inner door. Meanwhile, in this uproar, Cromwell and his officers were dining downstairs. Captured at last, Richard was going to be hanged when Sir Thomas Fairfax "who had a kindness for him, prevented it."[44]

· It is more probable that very little of the sort ever happened. A body of veteran troops would think nothing of clearing up small posts of resistance like Houndhill. The forty soldiers shrink into forty of Richard's tenants, probably hiding from the stories of the men of blood and iron. Even the parliamentarians in their accusations against Richard never suggested that he actually resisted them, and he himself subsequently swore that he "was never in Armes against the Parliament."[45] Knowing that his position was hopeless, Richard probably surrendered as soon as he was told to do so. The only truth in the romantic story, and that was true of a great deal of the time, was that his wife was either pregnant or recovering from the birth of a child.

Worsbroughdale being now overrun by parliamentarians, Richard decided to go to York, which still held out for the King, where his property was still his own and where still remained his lucrative office as deputy finer of Papists. He probably arrived there, one of an army of frightened and bewildered conservatives, towards the end of 1643. The army of Fairfax closed around the blockaded city which was under the command of the Marquess of Newcastle. Richard's neighbours and friends, Thomas Edmunds and Robert Rockley,[46] were

---

[43] At Wortley there was a comparatively large and strictly military garrison of 150 dragoons. *Hist. Wors.* p. 13.

[44] *Hist. Wors.*, p. 130, *et seq.*

[45] *Royalist Composition Papers.* Y.A.S. Records, vol. XV, p. 343.

[46] Robert Rockley was among the armistice Commissioners sent out on 16 June 1644 (*Newes from the Siege before Yorke.* 8vo. London, 1644), and again on 19 June (*The Kingdome's Weekly Intelligencer*, No. 60, June 1644). Nothing came of these meetings for the Royalists insisted on permission to march their army out to rejoin the King's forces.

also in the city and were among those who composed the articles for the surrender of the city.[47] On 20 June 1644, the day after the latest unsuccessful attempt to reach some mutually acceptable terms, the Roundheads sprang a mine they had been digging. St. Mary's Tower was torn apart in the explosion, together with scores of royalists and the ancient Worsbrough Manor records. The attackers were repulsed and the city did not finally surrender until 15 July 1644, when many of the defenders moved out to join the King's forces in Carlisle.

When this occurred Richard's position was not an enviable one, a relapsed malignant now a second time on the wrong side of the fence. His offices in the city were later broken into just as had been his office at Houndhill. Because of his subsequent complaints more is known about it:

> "One Captain William Beckwith, with a company of soldiers broke the Petitioner's studdy door in the said citty, and a great iron chest with seaven boults, and conveyed away all his writings there, and plundered his studdy."

By this time, however, Richard had hurried off. He heard later that when Beckwith and his company had done their worst, a whole crowd of Parliamentarian sequestrators for the city had pushed their way in and had taken away most of the papers that remained.[48]

When the city life came back to normal, the Committee of York, a many-headed parliamentarian town-major, ordered Richard to produce whatever documents both soldiers and sequestrators had left; he found nearly two thousand more papers which he handed over to the City Committee. Then the Roundhead authorities ordered him to make up his accounts for the years 1641 to 1643 inclusive. He had been promised temporary immunity so that his records of recusants' fines should be full and complete, but now he had absolutely no documents left to which he could refer. In his petition he begged Parliament therefore:

> "that he may be restored to the possession of his house and office in the citty, and to his library of bookes of accompts, chests and writings so conveyed away as aforesaid, whereby he may be enabled to conform with your honourable order."

The Parliamentary Committee referred this complaint to the sequestrators, who replied that Richard only wished to:

> "Disgrace them in the due execution of theire office . . . for which the said Elmhirst deserves severe and exemplaire punishment he and other of his servantes who are Enemies to the State"

that they, the sequestrators:

> "are much troubled that they should be enjoined to give answers to the articles exhibited by such a notorious delinquent, and one that absented himself from his own house, until of late that that he was informed that the King's party was to come for Yorkshire."

They go on to complain that Houndhill had largely escaped sequestration by Richard and his old mother pretending that much of it belonged to her, his

---

[47] *Hist. Wors.*, p. 33.
[48] *Hist. Wors.*, p. 132.

mother, as her jointure. Now Richard was treating Houndhill as his own again and:

"since upon the coming on of the King's party, the said Elmhirst has given away to the poor of Barnsley 8 acres of Oates and hath embezzled and wasted a great parte of his personal estate."

From his estate they had only sold a few loads of hay:

"and concerning the bookes, they say that the said Elmhirst had conveyed them out of his house, and hid them conningly in a private place in a swine stye."

Richard must have complained of the soldiers billeted in Houndhill and the damage they had done because they answer:

"as for keeping the soulders in his house necessitie caused it, fear of the enemy, Pontefract and Sandal being then the King's Garrisons and at liberty . . . The houndes and bowling allie in the articles mentioned—the hounds are kept by him, and the bowling allie made and maintained by him. These respondents think it most meete that such adjudged delinquents, who are enemies to the Commonwealth, that their persons should be secured, and for the doing thereof humbly praye the favour of the Board."[40]

This business was far from settled when Richard together with thousands of other "adjudged delinquents" was in even worse trouble. Parliament, in need of cash for the payment of its armies, particularly that of Scotland, started the great business of the Compositions. Under this scheme those Royalists who had had their estates sequestered, as had Richard, were to be fined in proportion to their offence and their estate. The committee in charge of this system of fines, sitting at the Goldsmiths Hall in London, began its work in July 1644. In March 1645 the powers of the committee were widened and Parliament gave it authority to summon any known malignant. Later that same year a scale of penalties was decreed, estates were to be compounded for a two years' estimated rent at pre-Civil War values and then, in addition to this fine on estates, Royalists had to pay an additional 10 per cent. of the value of their personal property, goods and chattels. As well as the material penalty they had to suffer a moral humiliation which most of them seemed not to mind: the compounder had to obtain leave of the Committee to be allowed so to compound and so not be liable to even greater penalties, when this permission to be fined had been allowed by the Committee, it was the responsibility of the compounder to make a complete list of all his properties, with their pre-war values set against each item, and together with this list he had to append a certificate from an "approved Minister" to say that he had taken the Roundheads' "National Covenant" and that he had "lived orderly since." Delinquents who so compounded after 1st December 1645 were not let off so lightly and fines were proportionately raised.

Three days before the expiry of the time limit, Richard, seeing no hope of the King's return to authority and the Civil War practically over, obediently

---

[40] *Hist. Wors.*, p. 133.

called at the Committee and begged permission to be allowed to compound for his sequestered estates. Next day he left his friends and took the Covenant.[50] On the 29th, with one day to spare, he took the last oath and, presumably, submitted the list of his properties, together with his pleas for various remissions he hoped to obtain. This list of his properties, together with their values, is still in existence.[51] But there exists in addition, as has already been described, his own catalogue of his properties which he drew up in 1638, in the immediate pre-war period in which the Commissioners were interested. Comparison of the two lists, the 1638 one absolutely correct and the one recalling 1640 for the benefit of the Commissioners of 1645, is very instructive. Richard admitted that his swollen properties now brought him in no less than £290 a year. Actually it was probably more than this; the Higham property which alone appears to be exactly the same, he valued at £20 a year in the privacy of his study, but called it £15 a year in front of the Commissioners. As well as his income from his lands, the gross value of his goods and chattels he placed at just over £50; he had in addition a most unexpected investment in "an old Adventure of seven tunne and a halfe in the Greenland Companye, the same worth £60." In other words, he admitted to being liable to fines of £580 (two years' rental) on his lands, and £11 (10 per cent. of his chattels); in all, some £591. To offset this, in addition to his complaints of all the damage and looting which his properties had undergone in the wars, he claimed to be allowed £20 a year fine-free, because this he paid to his mother[52] as her dower. Then there was another £30 a year which he said he paid to Elizabeth, widow of Francis Hemsworth, in lieu of her jointure: it is difficult to understand Richard's alleged responsibility here.[53] Lastly, he said that many of his lands he was merely holding as securities for a debt owed him by Sir George Radcliffe, and that many of his freehold lands, in Worsbrough and elsewhere, he had in reality made over to his father-in-law "for raisinge portions for my younger children."

The committee at Goldsmiths Hall seems to have been not unreasonable. Early in the new year[54] they had a note from their West Riding representatives which agreed that £20 a year should be excluded from the fineable total because this was paid to Richard's mother. In May 1646 he was still producing complaints and reasons as to why he should be excused more and more.[55] Someone called Willy was taking advantage of the turbulent times by keeping him out of some of his South Ottrington lands and even in Worsbroughdale Roger Genn had seized a messuage and lands from him. Against both these he was now about

---

[50] Before William Barton, the parson of [St.] John Zacharias.
[51] Y.A.S. Records, vol. XV, 1893.
[52] Buried 27 March 1647-1648. Wors. Par. Reg.
[53] She had been remarried to a Mr. Ellis, and lived in Fairburn Hall, part of the property for which Richard was compounding.
[54] 13 Jan. 1645/6. Y.A.S. Records, XV, p. 347.
[55] 22 May 1646. Ibid., p. 353.

to have a lawsuit and therefore requested that this should be taken into consideration. Richard may have been telling the truth: a discredited Royalist was an obvious target in those revolutionary days.

Richard's assessment was announced in the middle of 1646, the fine was placed at £566; he found a welcome cause of delay. A Parliament man called Henry Stewart had been granted £1,500 which was to come from the fine set on Sir George Radcliffe, who had been assessed as owner of Coulton. Radcliffe said that Elmhirst had compounded for at least part of Coulton and it was unreasonable that he, Radcliffe, should now be fined so heavily. Stewart, only interested in his £1,500, complained to the House of Lords.[56]

Eight months later Stewart was again asking their Lordships to assist him. This time he said that Elmhirst not only claimed half of Coulton, but threatened the tenants there that they should pay half their rent to him and that Stewart should never have more than the other half.[57] Richard answered, and it seems with justice, that half of the manor was his, he even sent a certificate from the Goldsmiths Hall commission to say that he had indeed compounded for the moiety of the disputed manor.

Radcliffe's personal opinion on the subject, in a letter written in Royalist exile in Rouen to a kinsman, still survives:

"I understand by a friend in England that Ric. Elmhurst is in suit with one Stewart, a sottish Irishman, about the manors of Colton and Fairburn: and I imagine that may be the reason why he has forborne now a good while to write unto me. So as right be done, it is not greatly material to me who prevails in this suit; in regard that I must pay them both their demands, what matter it who be paid first?

"But it may concerne you or yours to know how the case stands betwixt Richard Elmhurst and me, because next after my son, yr. wife is heir to my land. Thus therefore it is: when I bought those lands I had some money at my command in Ireland, which I was desirous to bestow in England. But for the present wanting in England some part of what I was to pay alderman Hoyle for Coulton, Ric. Elmhurst procured for me £2,000 and some odd money; which he might the more willingly trust me with because I had moneys in Ireland out of which I could repay this debt in a very few months. In the mean time I was content, and gave order that these two manors should be bought in his name, joined to another friend, whom I named for myself: so as the moiety thereof should be security for him, as well for that sum of £2,000 and odd moneys, as also for whatsoever other debts and accounts as there was one considerable account for which he stood engaged for me and as my surety. Besides, in recompense of his former service I promised to procure for him an office in York, which I made account would cost me £500. When I came to Ireland, after the purchase of Coulton, my Lord of Strafford made me join him in a bargain whereof my part cost me £17,500 a bargain which if the times had been good was likely to have been of great advantage; but these troubles in that kingdom have occasioned me loss more than I am willing to mention.

"This occasion took up all my money and brought me into a great debt, which presseth me to this hour, yet I was the less troubled for R. Elmhurst, because I knew he was well secured; and therefore providing for such debts as were likely to urge me more,

[56] House of Lords Calendar, 1646. Sept. 18. (Lords Journal, VIII, 496.)
[57] House of Lords Calendar, 1647. May 12. (Lords Journal, IX, 186.)

I never paid unto him any part of the prementioned £2,000 and odd moneys, but I still justly owe it; neither have I cleared my account for which he is bound, nor satisfied him that £500 which I was to have laid out for ye office, or in case the office could not be had, he was to have the money; for all which he hath not, nor ever had any other security than the moities of the manors aforesaid. I confess that I have not been fully satisfied with his estrangeing himself from me these late years; yet having formerly trusted him much, I never found him but an honest man: and I will not believe otherwise of him till I see the contrary. However it becomes me to do him and all them right, which is the reason why I write this much to you, not knowing how soon it may concern you; for I find age and infirmities come fast upon me, increased with want and many crosses, which daily put me in mind of my mortality."[58]

Stewart being very temporarily silenced and his own fines paid, Richard could breathe again, the worst apparently over. His name, among those of seventeen other Royalists, was passed through the House of Lords as "cleared of their delinquency."[59] But in the meantime Stewart had been maintaining a constant correspondence with the Upper Chamber about the unsatisfactory payment of rents from Coulton. A sidelight on this period is extracted from a letter from Thomas Edmunds of Worsbrough, Richard's friend and neighbour, co-Royalist and Lord of the Manor, to Sir Philip Percivall in London, dated 11 October 1647.[60] He wrote about his financial hardships and continued:

"Sir William Lister, Mr. Luke Robinson and Mr. Lionel Copley all owe me money, yet I dare not sue, they being Parliament men. I beseech you help a man that loves you truly.
"Postscript.—My loving neightbour, Mr. Elmhirst, has somewhat to do in the Parliament. I pray you bestead him in what you lawfully may."

It seems fair to assume that partisan justice, the scales tilted against Royalists, was employed against Richard on this occasion. Parliament decreed that all the rents of Coulton should be paid to Stewart. Next month it was Elmhirst's turn to complain to the Lords, repeating that he had paid no less than £320 of his composition because of his possession of half the manor of Coulton at Goldsmiths Hall and praying "that he and his tenants may not be disturbed in, much less divested of, their possession without legal trial."[61]

The bogus Houses of Lords and Commons had meanwhile set up a committee to enquire into the national revenue and among the other items was listed the income derived from recusants' rents. Sir George Wentworth, the arch-receiver, was ordered to produce his accounts for the years immediately preceding the Civil War. Messrs. Elmhirst, Raylton and Pulford were told to attend the committee and in the meantime not to dispose of any monies they held.[62] Exasperated, Richard subsequently petitioned Parliament, telling them how

[58] He did not die till 1657. (Sir Geo. Radcliffe to his brother. Rouen, March 1648.) This letter is addressed to John Hodgson of Beeston Park in Leeds, and not to Radcliffe's actual brother as stated in History of Worsbrough.
[59] House of Lords Calendar, 1647. Oct. 2. (Lords Journal, IX, 462.)
[60] Egmont MSS. Hist. MSS. Commission, vol. I, Part ii, p. 478.
[61] House of Lords Calendar, 1647. Nov. 11. (Lords Journal, IX, 518.)
[62] *Cal. State Papers. Domestic.* Chas. I. Vol. DXIV, No. 106. Dated 17 Dec. 1646.

ridiculous it was to expect him to produce accounts when both his offices, at York and Houndhill, had been so thoroughly ransacked and trampled over by Captain Beckwith and his clumsy troop.

The Parliament men, or, as Richard's son was to call them, "Oliver's Catchpoles," had other cards up their sleeves. The Government had set up another committee, "The Committee for the Advance of Money." It began its work by appealing for voluntary contributions. Presents being scarce and mean, the committee moved on to assessing contributions from rich men living within twenty miles of London. This, too, being exhausted, some sharp member suggested that those delinquents who, in compounding for their delinquencies, had concealed any part of their resources or their estate, should now be re-assessed and fined; this new rate was to be 5 per cent. of their personal estate.[63]

In the new year Richard found that his case had been reconsidered and he had been fined a further £300.[64] He complained that he had been already mulcted £566 for his composition at Goldsmiths Hall, of which £360 was for lands mortgaged by Sir George Radcliffe, for which he had been obliged to compound or lose his title, and four months afterwards those lands had been taken from him by a Parliament order. He had since sold land, for which he had paid £98 fine, in York City and County, and this had gone in paying another fine, settling his debts and in rebuilding his house at Houndhill, ruined by the wars. He was still more than £100 in debt. He had lost the profits of his lands during both sieges of Pontefract by the Parliament's forces taking free billets and free provisions, and he had had to pay towards the upkeep of Sir Edward Rhodes' light cavalry; might he therefore be excused from this further penalty?[65]

The Committee compromised with a fine of £100, only on the condition that this was settled within a month.[66] This was very promptly paid and Richard's £100, five days later, was directed into the pockets of an Oliver Cromwell. This particular man was a parliamentarian major £2,000 in arrears of pay, who was about to go to Ireland to join the army of his great Major-General namesake.[67] On 7 August 1650[68] Richard got his receipt for the second fine.

In the last year of his life, when Edmunds was still being pursued by the Commissioners, a London bookseller brought out a small octavo, full of errors, called a "Catalogue of the Lords Knights and Gentlemen than have compounded for their estates."[69] In the preface the editor insisted: "he hath no desire to revive your past misfortunes or to involve you in newe ones." Here Richard is listed as a Gentleman of Hamdill and is inaccurately rated as having been fined a total of £556.

[63] Calendar Proceedings Commission for Advance of Money, 1642-56.
[64] Calendar Proceedings Commission for Advance of Money, 1642-56. 29 Jan. 1647. Vol. 71, No. 57.
[65] Calendar Proceedings Commission for Advance of Money, 1642-56. 7 Dec. 1649. Vol. 110, No. 38.
[66] Calendar Proceedings Commission for Advance of Money, 1642-56. 7 Dec. 1649. Vol. 8, No. 51.
[67] Calendar Proceedings Commission for Advance of Money, 1642-56. 12 Dec. 1649. Vol. 8, No. 61.
[68] Hist. Wors., p. 142.
[69] Printed for Thomas Dring at "the signe of the George in Fleet Street neare Clifford Inne, 1655."

Thomas Wentworth's son, now the second Earl of Strafford, and wisely living in France, employed Richard, as his father had done, in the management of his Yorkshire affairs.   In a letter to his cousin, written from the exile Royalist centre of Rouen, where also died Sir George Radcliffe, the Earl writes concerning his future employment as agent:[70]

"I expect to hear of Ri. Elmust. If he sh'd not be able to attend on my occasions, I desire you will make choice of one that is honest and able; but if Ri. Elmust be willing, I desire you will forthwith instruct him as I have sett down."[71]

Edmunds, his neighbour and good friend at Worsbrough Hall, did not get free from the Commissioners until 1655.   But by the first day of 1647, two years before the King's execution, Edmunds had so far reconciled himself with the new regime that he had applied at the College of Arms for a grant of armorial bearings.   At that time the King's Heralds had been replaced by men favourable to the Parliament and these men, subsequently called usurpers, were fulfilling all the duties and responsibilities of their posts.   A grant of arms was made to Edmunds and it seems extremely probable that Richard bought one at the same time.   No full record of grants made during the heraldic usurpation have survived, but he certainly used, in the years before his death, a coat of arms which had never been granted to anybody else and which by its very structure suggests an expert hand.   A dozen years later, when the reinstated Royal Heralds made their visitation in Yorkshire, Richard was dead and his heirs, as will be seen, merely stated that the armorial bearings belonged to them and could or would produce no proof.

The remaining years of Richard's life appear to have been quietly devoted to the care of his own property, well out of the attention of the rulers of England. He served too as churchwarden.[72]

In 1651 he settled, once and for all, the rents and fines upon inheritance which had to be paid on his two copyhold premises of Elmhirst and Houndhill.   These had figured in the great trial of 1626, when dead John Booth's will had been invoked in favour of a reduced payment.   By an important deed dated 7 May 1651, Francis Rockley of Rockley, who had come into the rights of the manor, a stupid spendthrift man doomed to perish in a debtor's cell, bound himself and all subsequent Lords of the Manor never to demand a fine of more than two shillings on every admittance to Elmhirst and Houndhill and never more than thirteen shillings and fourpence on those occasions when the copyhold was forfeited to the lord for manorial offences.   At the same time this document settled the various fees liable on other fields more recently acquired from the manor.[73]

---

[70] The Earl had first tried to obtain the services of Thomas Edmunds, who was forced to decline the post: "I find my eyes as apt to fail me as any other organ, which had need be very good, if much employed in money matters, especially as the coyne of England is now clipped and counterfitted."   *Hist. Wors.*, p. 36.
[71] Earl of Strafford to Sir Geo. Wentworth of Wooley, 1 July 1648. *Hist. Wors.*, p. 142.
[72] *Hist. Wors.*, p. 312.
[73] Deed making certain the copyhold fines on Elmhirst and Houndhill. 7 May 1651. Elmhirst MSS.

Two years later, Richard wrote his will "being in perfect health and memory, praised be God." He here confirmed the arrangements he had already made concerning the hereditary lands, particularly Elmhirst and Houndhill. It was to be presumed that these were to pass in time to his eldest son, Richard, now a boy of thirteen. Most of the remainder of his extensive freehold property in Penistone, Hoyland Swaine, Bargh, Ardsley and Rothwell, he left to his widow and after her death or remarriage to his younger sons and unmarried daughters, who were, however, to make an annuity of £50 to her if she found a second husband. The other properties, Coulton, Fairburn, Wheledale and Darton, were left on trust to provide an income of £96 per annum for his younger sons and unmarried daughters until such time as the capital value of the property, £1,300, should be paid to them. Out of these properties, too, came a legacy of £500 to the Earl of Strafford and an unspecified amount to settle "any ingagement entered into with Sir George Radcliffe". The house in York, with its furnishings, was for his widow, while young Richard was to have:

> "all my goods, chattells and Household stuffe and implements of Husbandry in and about my House at Houndhill willing and desireing that the same shall and may remaine as heirelooms in and about the said House."[74]

Richard died in the autumn of 1654 at his house in York, being buried with Margaret the shining star in the church of St. Helens,[75] on 31 October 1654.

---

[74] Somerset House. Vol. "Berkeley," folio 171. 31 Dec. 1653.
[75] The funeral is entered on the register of Holy Trinity in York with the comment, "buried at St. Ellens."

GENERATION X

THOMAS ELMHIRST OF BOSTON
1649-1697

One of the first duties of Elizabeth, Richard's widow, was to go to London to prove her husband's will. During the ten years of the Commonwealth, it was ordered that wills from all over England should be proved in the metropolis instead of in the local Diocesan Courts. In this, as in so many other ways, the new republic was many centuries in advance of its times: the Principal Probate Registry was not to be re-established in London for two more centuries. So, on 17 May 1656, Elizabeth was granted administration of her husband's property. Two years later she obtained the original will from London, where only a copy remains.[1]

Elizabeth had a large family on her hands. Richard the eldest boy was fifteen,[2] William was ten, Thomas, from whom all living Elmhirsts are descended, was only six,[3] and John, unless he had already died, was three. In addition to the boys there were five girls. It was fortunate that there was so much money even after a year's time, when their income was reduced. By an indenture in 1657, Elizabeth, the widow, together with her daughter Eleanor, presumably the eldest, agreed with the trustees to accept only £78 per annum from the Coulton property, which had been conveyed to Thomas Radcliffe, instead of the £96 yearly which had been fixed by Richard in his will. Since this annual income was to be derived from a capital value of £1,300, the new rate seems to have been more reasonable, representing 6 per cent. interest. This £78 was to be remitted to the widow by Radcliffe in her dwelling-house in York City in two half-yearly sums, in February and August, until the capital was paid.[4] The chief interest in this document lies below the signatures of Elizabeth and Eleanor. They both employed the seal which must have been used by Richard and which shows the family arms in their present-day form. These arms, Barry wavy of six and a canton paly wavy of six, were impressed from what must have been a signet ring.[5] Unfortunately both seals are broken but enough remains to be certain of the armorial charges.

Elizabeth Elmhirst received few such payments. Later this same year she died in York and was buried at St. Helens. In her will she left the greater part of her personal possessions equally among her younger children. Three green

---

[1] Somerset House, Vol. "Berkeley," folio 171. Note dated 15 Dec. 1658.
[2] Bapt. 1 Jan. 1640. Wors. Par. Reg.
[3] Bapt. 24 Jan. 1649. Wors. Par. Reg.
[4] Indenture dated 10 Sept. 1657.
[5] Widow Elizabeth subsequently bequeathed to her son Richard "his father's gold ring" and to her son Thomas "his father's silver seale."

carpets, the chairs and the green bed which had been moved to the York house from Houndhill, were returned to her eldest son. She mentions two other Elmhirsts about whom nothing is known; her son, Robert, who must have died very young; and "To Richard Elmhirst, goldsmith, 40s. to set up his trade when he begins to trade for himself, and then to be paid him." Bequests are also made to the poor of Worsbrough, Barnsley and the village of Haxby, from which she had come as a bride.[6]

The careers of the three surviving boys were destined to be very different. Richard, as head of the family and the eldest son, was to stay on the ancestral lands. William, the second son, became a doctor, and Thomas, the third, as was so frequent with younger landless brothers, entered the business world in some, as yet, unspecifiable trade.

Soon after the Restoration of King Charles, Richard got himself a wife, he being then just come of age.[7] He married a girl called Alice Dickson from Darfield close by. Next year their first child, a daughter Elizabeth, was baptised in Worsbrough.[8]

Meanwhile, brother William had gone up to Clare Hall, Cambridge, to start his medical studies. Thomas, too, would probably not be considered too young to begin his mercantile apprenticeship. Their sister Elizabeth, now aged twenty-two, married Edward Canby, of Thorne[9]; two relics of this marriage survive, pieces of Carolean silver engraved with the arms of Canby impaling those of Elmhirst, each within a sweeping cartouche; the Canby achievement incidentally being as little sanctioned by the reformed College of Arms as was that of Elmhirst.

In 1665 occurred the last of the heraldic visitations of Yorkshire. These had been instituted in early Tudor times to tax or to curb the presumptuous rising middle class and also, more laudably, as an attempt to record pedigrees which would otherwise have been lost. By the time of this last visitation the method had lost much of its ferocity. But still the technique remained the same; summonses were sent out by the representative of the visiting officer of the College of Arms to all those who either used coats-of-arms, or who looked as though they might so use them if they had the opportunity.[10] Such people were expected to appear at some local centre, in this particular case the Star Inn at Barnsley, on a certain date, for Richard Elmhirst it was 5 August 1665.

Those so summoned who claimed the right to arms were expected to bring

---

[6] *Abstracts of Yorkshire Wills*, 1655-6. Y.A.S. Record Series, vol. IX, p. 114. Proved by Ellen Elmhirst, 21 Nov. 1657.
[7] Paver's "Marriage Licences," 1661.
[8] 2 Dec. 1661. Wors. Par. Reg.
[9] Paver's "Marriage Licences," 1663.
[10] What appears to be an original list of those to be summoned is in the Brit. Mus. (MS. 12482). Richard Elmhirst is not in this collection of names, but it includes John Wordsworth, of Worsbrough, who was subsequently disqualified.

with them evidence of their right, whether in the form of a previous grant to an ancestor in the male line, or else "ancient usage," which to this particular herald, Dugdale, Norroy King of Arms, meant a demonstration of the fact that these arms had been in use in the family for a hundred years or more. Men who had used arms without proof either of grant or of ancient custom, were liable to one of three penalties. They might admit their wrong and apply forthwith for an official grant; they might, and some with justice, reiterate their claim and beg for leave to show their proofs on another occasion, in which case they were usually given a time limit to show them at the College of Arms in London, or, as a last alternative, the brazen and obviously illegal bearer, who was not prepared to purchase a grant, was subject to all the penalties of heraldic wrath: such men could be compelled to have their false arms erased wherever they had been put, whether on silver, tombstones or stained glass, and in addition they had to suffer their ignoble and ungentlemanly names being published in the local market town. Doubtless the fear of this shame drove many to ask for grants, to the benefit of the visiting herald, the College of Arms and their own descendants.

When Richard, as head of the family, though only twenty-five years of age, went to the Star Inn, he took with him the parchment pedigree that his father had had prepared. On the same occasion present at the inn with varying emotions of self-satisfaction, pride, uncertainty and frank dismay, were almost a dozen others of the gentry or near-gentry. Five men that day had their pedigrees recorded: Beale of Woodhouse, only four generations but six armorial quarterings; William Lister, of Thornton, and Sir John Kay, of Woodsome, both with short pedigrees, but both with fashionably quartered arms. Mr. Nevill, from Chevet, shaming them all with his ancient simple red saltire on a silver shield; and lastly, old Captain Monkton, from Hodroyd, a man of no lineage but a tried Royalist of the Civil War, who was not even certain what the arms were that he claimed, but who was nevertheless recorded with the best. However doubtful Richard may have been about the authority for his coat of arms at least none of the others, not even Sandford Nevill, showed so long a pedigree. The remainder of those who attended the summons could not prove their claim to gentle blood though the final list of those so publicly disgraced was not published until three years later when presumably all false claims had been investigated; then Dugdale wrote to the High Sheriff of Yorkshire enclosing their names for public condemnation. Staincross Wapentake alone contained seventeen of these unfortunates.[11] Dugdale accepted the family pedigree as it was written and this in itself is a good indication as to its value since he was one of the most accurate and painstaking of the antiquarian scholars of his age. The arms were recorded, with the difference of a plain canton sable, and under the shield was written, "These arms respited", to signify that Richard asked for

---

[11] Nov. 1668. *Dugdale's Vis. York.* Surtees Soc., vol. XXXVI, p. xiii.

time in which to demonstrate his right. When a fair copy came to be made for the permanent records at the College of Arms the words "Nothing Done" had been added. So Richard had failed to make his proof, which in any case could not have been of ancient usage since none had used the arms before his father. Dugdale was willing to accept as valid any arms if they had been used from the beginning of Queen Elizabeth's reign. That is to say, that he, unlike modern Kings of Arms, recognised arms which had been borne without official sanction for about a century, providing, of course, that they were not already the arms of somebody else.[12] If Richard's claim was by grant, as seems most probable, it would have been by a grant from the usurping heralds during the Commonwealth period, a fact of which he would not have been proud in these immediate post-Restoration years. It is quite possible, however, that Richard had no idea of the grounds for his father's use of the arms since he was too young when his father died to have either understood or cared.

Henry Edmunds, his neighbour from Worsbrough Hall, had the advantage of being older than Richard, and he knew that his own father had had a grant soon after the Civil War had finished.[13] He decided to admit this fact. Norroy Dugdale could not recognise such an authorisation from the parliamentarian College of Arms and so subsequently made a new grant.[14]

In 1670 Richard's younger brother, William, obtained his bachelor's medical degree at Cambridge: there is no way of telling where he practised in the earlier part of his life; he had certainly come back to Worsbrough before he was forty. Still less can be found about the early days of the youngest brother, Thomas, a merchant at Boston, in Lincolnshire.

Compared with the energy and pushfulness of his father, Richard, living at Houndhill, a peaceful young man, led a lazy, uneventful life. He had altogether four children, of whom only a boy and girl, Joshua and Elizabeth, grew out of childhood. What exactly happened at Houndhill is not known. When only thirty-four years old, Richard fell ill, made his will[15] and died.[16] Before many more months had passed his young wife was also dead.[17] The property came to the children—Joshua, aged four, and Elizabeth, aged eleven. It is very probable that their senior uncle, Dr. William, now came to live in Worsbrough-dale to manage the affairs of the estate as their guardian.

Death, unexpected death, was to alter the fate of Houndhill yet again. In August 1683, young Joshua, then a boy of fourteen, sickened and died. Buried

---

[12] Letter from Dugdale to Wm. Horsley, 15 June 1668. Lansdown MS. 870, folio 88. Printed in *Ancestor*, vol. 2, p. 45.
[13] 1 Jan. 1647. Joseph Foster, *County Families of Yorkshire*, vol. I, 1874.
[14] *Dugdale's Visit. York.* Surtees Soc., vol. XXXVI, p. 9.
[15] 12 Feb. 1673. York Registry, vol. 55, folio 26.
[16] Buried 1 Mar. 1673. Wors. Par. Reg.
[17] Buried 21 June 1673. Wors. Par. Reg.

in Worsbrough Church, a brass which still remains was engraved to his memory.[18] His sister Elizabeth now became a wealthy heiress and on 11 October 1683 she was admitted (as well as she could be, being still only twenty years old) to Houndhill, Ouslethwaite and Bankhouse. Such a girl, had she had the figure of a hippopotamus and the features of a warthog, would not long have remained unmarried in the seventeenth century. Within a few months she was betrothed to John Copley, of Nether Hall, in Doncaster; with him she leaves the story, taking with her nearly all the fortune amassed by Richard her grandfather.

By mediaeval custom a female serf marrying out of the manor relinquished her holdings there to her nearest male relative. Elizabeth may have been bound by this custom or else may have deliberately willed that her copyhold properties in Worsbrough pass to her Uncle William, now the head of the family. On 23 May 1684, she made a formal surrender "to the hands of the Lady of the Manor by a straw" of the messuages of Elmhirst, occupied by a John Turton, and the other places, including Genn House, where now dwelt Doctor William Elmhirst, Gentleman. On the same day seisin of all these properties was granted to the doctor who did the traditional fealty for them. All the rest of Elizabeth's lands being now tied up by a bevy of prosperous referees, Sir Godfrey Copley, Henry Edmunds from the Manor, and George Sitwell, her betrothed's relative from Renishaw, she was shortly thereafter married.[19]

Elmhirst certainly came to Doctor William, but there seems to have been some complication with regard to Houndhill. Since it was undoubtedly copyhold of the manor, it would be expected to go to him as the senior Elmhirst, and indeed he probably lived there for the next fifteen years.[20] But after that, however, it surprisingly followed Elizabeth to the Copleys. Possibly Elizabeth had arranged to buy her childhood home from the manor, with the permission of the lord. Then, for as long as was convenient, or as long as she was alive, it could be occupied by her uncle.

With the young head of the family dead, the heiress married, the confirmed bachelor doctor living in Houndhill, and Thomas, the younger uncle, still unmarried and immersed in business affairs, the family showed every sign of dying out. It is due to Thomas, of Boston, that it still continues. His history was closely interwoven with the story of the times and in particular with the attempts of tyrant Stuarts to model themselves on the ruling despot of France, whose money and religious prejudices they shared.

---

[18] Under the face of a cherub with curly hair and a gumboil are the words:
"Joshua unicus filius
Richardi Elmhirst de
Houndhill Gener: obijt
Vicessimo secundo die
Augusti Anno Domini
1683 et Aetatis decimoquarto."

[19] Married 12 Feb. 1683. Wors. Par. Reg.

[20] But in 1687 the Town Accounts for Sheffield record the payment of threepence "for sending a letter to Lees Hall [a mile or two south of Leeds] for Doctor Elmhurst." (John Leader: *Records of the Burgery of Sheffield*. London, 1897.)

Charles II, towards the end of his reign, had revenged himself on the Whigs by the confiscation of all the major city and borough charters. These were to be returned, sooner or later, with new regulations attached that made a working Whig majority an impossibility. The king's death brought no change. James II held similar views as his brother; not, like Charles, leavening the tyranny with personal charm and intelligence, but with his own peculiar brand of obtuseness and bigotry.

Thomas Elmhirst was never a freeman of Boston,[21] but in March 1685, a month after the new king's accession, he got his first official appointment in the borough, when he was appointed as an assistant to the Treasurer.[22] A few months later he was elected a Common Councillor and his future seemed assured. From his subsequent history it can safely be assumed that he obtained these important posts because of his known Tory leanings and his zeal for the Crown. This same year, at the age of thirty-two (1685), Thomas got himself married at Stixwould to Ann Bolton,[23] a Lincolnshire girl, who was twenty-three that year.

The Council of the Borough of Boston met on an average once a fortnight. Both Councillors and Aldermen were absent as frequently as they were present and Thomas was no more enthusiastic than his fellows. Most of such meetings dealt with leases of the town's property, collecting of rents and matters of order and local government.

Next month Thomas, probably with a sense of nothing but devout loyalty to King James, saw the emasculated charter of the town's liberties returned:
"At this Assembly the Charterbook was brought into the house with the translated Coppy of the new Charter by the Town Clerk."[24]

In yet another month Thomas and Ann had had their first child, a son named William,[25] probably after his uncle, the physician.

Tory Thomas was on the crest of the wave. Before he had been a Common Councillor for a twelvemonth, he was ahead of his seniors. The Council Minutes record:
"At this Assembly Tho. Elmhurst Gent. one of the Comon Counsell of this Borr. was Elected an Alderman in the room of Sr. Charles Dymoke Knt. a late Alderman of this Borr. decd. who 1st. took the Oathe of Allegiance [to the king] and supremacy [of the crown over the Church of England] & ye oathe mentioned in the late Article for regulating of Corporations [by which the king could not be opposed] & subscribed ye Test [to show that he was a member of the national church] & then took ye Oathe of Alderman of this Borr."[26]

---

[21] Unfortunate, for his occupation would have been recorded.
[22] 5 Mar. 1685. (Boston Council Minutes, folio 121.)
[23] Her descent from many prosperous Lincolnshire families is given in *Lincolnshire Pedigrees.* Harl. Soc., vol. L, pp. 164 and 232; vol. LII, p. 1023, quoting Coll. Arm. MS. C.23.
[24] 28 Sept. 1686. (Boston Council Minutes.)
[25] Bapt. 21 Oct. 1686. Boston Church Register.
[26] 11 Feb. 1687. (Boston Council Minutes, folio 129.)

By these oaths new aldermen bound themselves spiritually, for the Papist king was head of the Church, and temporarily, by the regulating article, to the absolute dictatorship of the king. Next month more rewards came Thomas's way and he was made Chamberlain, or Borough Treasurer, with an assistant to help him "in gathering up of the outrents."[27] He was now responsible for all the town's financial affairs, for the gathering of dues on market days, and the collection of all fees due to the corporation.

Thomas, and others like him all over the country who had been so rapidly promoted for their loyalty and reliability, was now to learn the trustworthiness of princes. The king, finding his schemes still opposed throughout the kingdom, ably assisted by Sunderland, decided to ensure liberty of worship to the Roman Catholics by pretended concern for liberty of all consciences everywhere. By the Declaration of Indulgence all penalties were lifted from the Dissenters and, as though by accident, the Romanists were set free from the repressions under which they had suffered for so long. The king wished to cement an unnatural union between Puritan and Papist in a determined attempt to convert the Established Church into a minority. One of the first moves on which the Court decided was another attempt to pack town corporations with either Roman Catholics or, since this was less likely to cause trouble, with Nonconformists, whom the king thought could so be flattered to become his allies.

On 23 March 1688 a conference was held at Whitehall to consider this new attempt to divide and conquer. Letters were despatched to most of the major corporations, making use of the new charters under which the king had given himself sufficient authority, ordering the dismissal of loyal churchmen. Boston's letter was among those sent out that spring:

"At the Court at Whitehall ye 23 day of March 1687 [1688]
   "Whereas by the Charter granted to the Town of Boston in the County of Lincoln a power is reserved to his Maty. by his order in Councill to remove from their employment any officer in the said Towne, his Maty. in Councill is pleased to order & it is hereby ordered that Thomas Barker, John Christopher & Mr. Thom. Elmhurst Aldermen [and various councillors] be & they are hereby removed & displaysd from their aforesaid offices in the sd. Town of Boston."

This notice of dismissal was read at the next Council meeting and dutifully incorporated, for there was now no alternative, into the town minutes.[28] Thomas had lost his honours even faster than he had obtained them, their loss in such circumstances did him no discredit. Officially written the day after the Whitehall conference, the second of the royal commands, the next letter, signed personally by the gloomy despot, was read out at the same Council meeting:

   "James R.
   "Trusty & welbeloved We greet you well. Whereas we have by our order in

---

[27] 25 March 1687. (Boston Council Minutes, folio 129.) Keys of the Treasury delivered to him 20 May 1687.
[28] 10 April 1688. (Boston Council Minutes, folio 137.)

Councell thought fitt to remove Thomas Barker, John Christopher & Thom. Elmhurst from being Aldermen [and various councillors] of our said Burrough. We have thought fitt hereby to will and require you forthwith to admitt & elect our trusty & welbeloved John Woods, Richard Roads & Willm. Pestor to be Aldermen [and others to be councillors] of our said Burrough in the room of the persons above menconed without administring unto them any oath for the execucon of their respective places wth. wch. we are pleased to dispence in this behalf & for so doing this shall be your Warrant.

"And so we bid you farewell. Given at our Court of Whitehall the 24 day of March 1687 [1688] in the fourth year of our Reign.

By his Majesties Comand,

Sunderland P.

Burrough of Boston.''

The rest of the story is national rather than personal; at least it made no difference to Thomas. King James pushed gloomily from folly to folly in the few months that remained to him. Macaulay wrote:

"Everywhere from the Tweed to the Lands End, Tory functionaries were ejected; and the vacant places were filled with Presbyterians, Independents and Baptists . . . The regulators indeed found that, in not a few places, the change had been for the worse. The discontented Tories, even while murmuring against the king's policy, had constantly expressed respect for his person and his office, and had disclaimed all thought of resistance. Very different was the language of some of the new members of corporations. It was said that old soldiers of the Commonwealth, who, to their own astonishment and that of the public, had been made Aldermen, gave the agents of the Court very distinctly to understand that blood should flow before Popery and arbitrary power were established in England.''[29]

It is interesting to note that Pestor, who had supplanted Thomas Elmhirst, was so bad a choice from the point of view of King James that he was made Mayor of Boston in the first year of William and Mary.[30]

Thomas continued to call himself Alderman and was busy at home. A second son, Richard, and four daughters, one a year, followed the birth of William. Only the last of the girls, Elizabeth[31] and Anne,[32] lived to marry. Then came a third son, Thomas.[33] Such fertility proved too much even for a young woman: three months after having Thomas, his mother died.[34]

Sometime within those years the Alderman had found time from his town business and his wife took time from among her pregnancies to sit for their portraits. They were probably painted by one of the second-rate itinerant artists who then toured the countryside, as they continued to do for the next century, offering to make likenesses, on canvas for comparatively small fees. A town alderman, even out of office, would be as much of a sitting target for such painters as are Lord Mayors to the modern academician. About the same

---

[29] Ld. Macaulay: *History of England.* II, p. 85 *et seq.* Longmans, 1866.
[30] 25 Mar. 1688 [1689]. (Boston Council Minutes.)
[31] Bapt. 17 Nov. 1690.
[32] Bapt. 1 Oct. 1689.
[33] Bapt. 6 Dec. 1692.
[34] Died 23 Feb. 1693 [1694]. Buried as "Mrs. Anne Elmast", 24 Feb. (Boston Church Reg.)

time as these portraits were commissioned two of the children were also portrayed in separate pictures in the pseudo-classical style so much in fashion in London twenty years before. In 1692, William, the eldest son, would have been six years old and one of the portraits is possibly his, the other may be of his brother Richard.[35]

Less than three years after his wife's death, Thomas the Alderman, his life perhaps shortened by the screaming of seven children all under ten years of age, fell mortally ill. On 28 January 1696 [1697], he made his will, which does not seem to have survived, and on the same day surrendered a small copyhold property with its orchard to the Steward of the Manor of Stonehall in Frampton, just outside Boston. He was not living there at the time; on the back of the deed of surrender is a relevant extract from his will by which he bequeaths this Frampton copyhold property to his second son, Richard, according to the terms of the lost testament and, of course, subject to its being regranted to him according to the custom of the manor.[36]

Five days later Thomas died.[37] He was buried by his young wife in Boston Church, where brasses on the north side of the chancel still remain to their memory.[38]

---

[35] William Elmhirst (1799-1864) wrote that they are Thomas and Richard, as the "eldest son Wm. who came into Yorkshire was not taken", but he gave no reason for making this statement. Both portraits are so alike that exact identification would not seem important.

[36] Egerton MS. 2996, folio 66 (Brit. Mus.). This surrender is sealed with the Elmhirst arms as they are now used.

[37] Died, says his memorial, 2 Feb. 1696 [1697] and buried the same day, according to the Parish Register.

[38] Placed so high that they are impossible to decipher without a ladder or the aid of field-glasses.

GENERATION XI

WILLIAM ELMHIRST OF LIVERPOOL AND ELMHIRST
1686-1746

William, the eldest of the many tow-headed orphans left in Lincolnshire, was only ten years old when his father died. It is not clear who looked after this numerous family left in the Alderman's house at Boston. Uncle William, the physician, may have cared for them as he had done for his other brother's children till death and matrimony had released him from those responsibilities. Alternatively, it may have fallen to the duty of the Boltons, the children's maternal aunts and uncles, a quantity of whom lived nearby,[1] to act as foster-parents. Before many years young William was probably apprenticed, his late father's business associates would have been useful, to a merchant in either Boston or Liverpool: this latter place is the more probable because it was here, once he was free of his apprenticeship, that he set up in business for himself.

Uncle William over at Houndhill was about this time deeply involved in a legal dispute with his sister, who had married Hastings Rasby, and more particularly with her son Richard Rasby. William's brother-in-law, Hastings, had borrowed and not repaid £500 before his death,[2] but in his will[3] he had directed that his two brothers-in-law, William the physician, and Thomas, the now dead Alderman, should be empowered as trustees to sell enough of the Rasby lands to enable this £500 to be returned to the physician. By such selling, £200 was raised and instantly used to settle even more pressing debts; thereafter the widow did all she could to prevent any more selling of land and "by faire speeches and other insinuatinge wayes" persuaded her brothers to wait until her son was twenty-one. In the meantime the boy had been apprenticed by the uncles to an apothecary, they chose the particular one employed by his uncle William. When he came of age the mother persuaded her brother to hand over the writings concerning the debt and gave in exchange a bond from the young man for £300 and a mortgage of some lands, valued at £10 per annum, for the remaining £200. Things might have remained relatively simple except that young Richard Rasby now began "makeinge his addresse to a gentlewoman whoe was an heiress and of a considerable fortune". A joineture being demanded by the girl's family, Richard persuaded his mother to make over her own jointure to his future wife in return for a guaranteed £30 a year from the property he had now inherited. This settled, young Richard married[4] "and haveinge contracted a greate many debts by his courtshippe and other his extravagant

---

[1] *Lincolnshire Pedigrees*, Harl. Soc., vol. 50, pp. 164 and 232, quoting Coll. Arm. MS. C.23.
[2] March 1677.
[3] Dated at York, 4 March 1675. (*The Genealogist*, vol. I, 1877, p. 96.)
[4] Married in 1695 to Elizabeth, widow of Richard Meager. (*The Genealogist*, vol. I, p. 96. 1877.)

wayes of liveinge" ceased to pay his mother the annuity that he had promised. She, poor widow, having no other means of support, appealed to her brother, the physician at Houndhill, who saw to it that she had "meate drinke and other neccessaries" during this difficult time. William now demanded that the debt of £500, nearly a quarter of a century overdue, should really be settled at last. Chancery proceedings were started. Richard Rasby's defence was not convincing. He was only seven years old when his father had died, but he remembered his uncle Thomas selling some of his father's lands. He had been bound apprentice when he was seventeen and had still three or four more years to serve even now that he had come of age. While assisting in his master's shop, his mother had come in with his uncle William, an attorney trailing behind them; two documents had been put in front and he had been ordered to sign "which this defendant understood not, haveinge no skill in things of that nature, yet not daring to refuse for fear of their anger." Thus, young Rasby claimed, the bond and the mortgage had been got out of him "by surprise". He went on to add, showing that however unworldly he may have been, at least he had some skill in things of that nature, that his father had left debts of only about £900 and that if that figure was now swollen to £1,200, that could only be due to the mismanagement of his affairs by his mother and his wicked uncles.

Richard Rasby's widowed mother, in her evidence, was obviously torn between her gratitude to her brother and her tried affection for her son. She agreed that her brother William was owed the money, but on the other hand, and it seems reasonable, she thought that at the time that the boy's signature had been obtained in the apothecary's shop, that there had been a certain pressure applied, particularly because the lad's master was employed by her brother.[5] The result of this lawsuit cannot be discovered. In the summer of the next year the Rasbys were ordered to complete their answers which had been due by a specified time. They were technically arrested and released on bail, being then permitted to make their answer in Yorkshire to save them the expense and trouble of coming to London.[6] This answer does not seem to be extant and the absence of any legal decision more than a year later suggests that the dispute was settled out of court.

Eighteen months after the lawsuit, William Elmhirst, the physician, made his will,[7] "being in perfect health and memory" and calling himself "late of Houndhill", as though in those months he had moved away from the house,[8] which was now to pass out of the family possession for more than two centuries,[9]

---

[5] P.R.O. Chancery Proceedings, C8.569/104. 22 Nov. 1700 onwards.
[6] P.R.O. Chancery decision vol. for 1701, folio 220. 7 May.
[7] Dated 10 July 1702. (Elmhirst MS.)
[8] In the Land Tax assessment for 1708, Houndhill is occupied by Richard Saltonstall (*Hist. Wors.*, p. 347). In his will in 1765 Robert Copley, Elizabeth Elmhirst's grandson, leaves it with everything else to his bastard son, then at Cambridge, Thomas Copley, alias Newby. This Thomas had an only son, another Thomas, who died unmarried. (Will of Robt. Copley, 15 July 1765.)
[9] Regained by Leonard Elmhirst in 1932.

to the new Genn House that he had rebuilt. In this testament he asked to be buried:

> "if I dye in or near Houndhill, in the North Alley in the Chappell of Worsbrough where my relations are buried; or if I die near York it may be buried in St. Helen's Church in Stonegate where my Father and Mother was buried. And concerning my worldly estate I give and bequeath to my nephew William Elmhirst (eldest son to my brother Thomas Elmhirst of Boston) the messuages or tenements . . . called Elmhirst . . . and Ouslethwaite.[10] . . all of which my neece Elmhirst left me before her marriage."

The other orphans at Boston were not forgotten; they received varying amounts of land or property, including the lands in Womersley which had been "mortgaged to me by sister Rasby and her son Richard for the payment of two hundred pounds." Even his youngest nephew was to get a lump sum of £200.

> "I give and bequeath my study of books with the chest they are in to any of the three sons [of my brother Thomas of Boston] that shall turn student in either of the two universitys or be an Apothecary or Chyrurgeon, otherwise I give them to my nephew John Lamb Chyrurgeon as fittest for his use; I give and bequeath to my nephew William my white Camblett Cloak, my best silver-hilted sword and pistolls and gun; And to Richard my other silver-hilted sword and my hanger to Thos. Elmhirst."

His Elmhirst nieces got silver tumblers; the unpleasant apothecary's apprentice, Richard Rasby, and his mother figured merely among the recipients of guineas with which to buy mourning rings. The good physician was not to die for another thirteen years.[11] He was buried neither at Worsbrough nor in York, but in the ancient church at Newark, where his Latin epitaph proclaimed his virtues:

He was of his God, King, Country and of his Friends

Whilst he lived a faithful & diligent Cultivator

Therefore

By all good men regretted he died

By none more than by the Poor

To whom Council & Medicine

He gratuitously administered.

Gracious God

May the tilled land of this kind of man be very

Fruitful.[12]

---

[10] Elmhirst was at this time leased to a man called John Tirton, and Ouslethwaite to a John Woodhead, these two properties with adjacent fields brought in an income of more than £40 a year. Both these places, being copyhold, belonged to the manor and would automatically have been regranted to young William in any event.

[11] 23 Dec. 1715 (Monumental Inscription). That same year he had had to give sixteen guineas, assessed as owner of Genn House, towards the support of Footsoldiers raised to repulse the Old Pretender. (Worsbrough Parish Accts., vol. 1693, p. 106.)

[12] No trace of this grave could be found in 1949, when the tombstones were being rearranged. An imperfect Latin transcription and an English translation remain among the family records.

The old doctor's nephew and heir was nearly thirty years old at this time and established in his merchant's business in Liverpool. Now made independent by his uncle's bequests, he married a girl in Worsbrough, Martha, one of the daughters of Robert Allot, of Lewdine,[13] and the ceremony took place at Silkstone Church, within three months of the old man's death.[14] William's younger brother, Richard, died the same year; all that is known is that he was lost at sea on a journey back from Virginia. It is likely that he was acting for his brother in Liverpool. William's prospects in the world of commerce seem to have vanished about the same time as his brother. There is evidence that William himself was also shipwrecked and he is reported as plaintively remarking in after years that if he and his ship "had got safe home, he would have been too worldly from his Riches".[15] This fate being successfully avoided, William seems to have kept well away from Liverpool. In their early years of married life he and his wife lived in the small house at Elmhirst and in 1723 they moved to Genn House,[16] which was to be their home for the rest of their lives. Punctually within a year of their marriage, his wife, Martha, produced their first child, a daughter Sarah, baptised at Worsbrough.[17] Another daughter, Ann, followed.[18] The growing family was made certain of its accommodation in church by William, petitioning to erect a family pew in the north-western corner of the building, where it still remains: "A certain seat . . . lately erected and built containing in length two and a half yards and in width two yards and four inches or thereabouts . . . for the purpose of sitting kneeling praying and hearing divine worship therein"[19]; the actual site for the pew seems to have been bought from the Cutler family and a Diocesan Decree was then requested to confirm the transaction.[20] The original woodwork panelling that survives is likely to be that erected in 1720, even though the interior of Worsbrough Church was twice enthusiastically renovated by the Victorians.[21]

From this period comes the first recorded reference of direct family profit from the hidden wealth of coal which was to enrich the Elmhirsts and their descendants. In 1718 Worsbrough old town account books noted the payment of seventeen shillings to Mr. Elmhirst for four loads of coal.[22] Such a transaction suggests a more efficient method than the digging from surface outcrops that

[13] William acquired no living father-in-law, and his mother-in-law, Sarah Allott, had already had a second family by a second husband, Francis Hall of Swaith; she had taken with her all her late husband's property, only one caudle cup being for some reason excluded, in exchange for a jointure that her new husband agreed to settle upon her. Agreement dated 28 April 1696. (Elmhirst MS.)
[14] 13 March 1715/16. Silkstone Par. Reg.
[15] Evidence of Lawrence Dyer, aged 71, in 1829. But another family record (Dr. Richard Elmhirst, about 1830) says that all William's profits were lost on the return journey from the East Indies.
[16] Evidence of Dr. Richard Elmhirst, about 1836.
[17] Bapt. 9 Feb. 1716/17. Wors. Par. Reg.
[18] Bapt. 24 June 1719. Wors. Par. Reg.
[19] Decree dated 11 Aug. 1720. (Elmhirst MS.)
[20] Notes on back of Decree, dated 1766.
[21] 1838 and 1864—"they are now pulling the old church at Worsbro' to pieces", wrote William Elmhirst on 4 Sept. 1838, when he had seen the family graves broken open and his brothers' coffins exposed.
[22] Hist. Wors., p. 248.

had got Robert Elmhirst into trouble exactly a hundred years before. By the early eighteenth century superficial mining had become general in the district; perpendicular shafts were not sunk as at present, but gently sloping inclines, known as day holes, were excavated and down these the miners walked to reach the coal face just underground. Coal rights were usually let out to individuals or small groups of miners, who, with the primitive means at their disposal, hardly did more than supply their own and their neighbours' needs. The state of the roads did not permit wholesale carriage of coals and the canals had yet to appear.

William's only son was baptised at Worsbrough on 29 December 1719, and was named, without much imagination, William.[23] For the next ten years very little seems to have happened to William[24] and his growing family. He was churchwarden twice.[25] Another daughter, Martha,[26] was born, and in 1737, for some unrecorded reason, he had to make a token surrender of all his copyhold lands to the Lord of the Manor.[27] Elmhirst and its surrounding fields then totalled some sixty-two acres and Genn House, where they lived, only eight or nine acres. After this surrender and a recital of the extent of the properties, they were handed back to William.[28]

In the fullness of time William's eldest daughter married Robert Greaves, of Clayton Hall, and shortly afterwards his wife Martha died.[29] William junior had meanwhile been apprenticed to an apothecary surgeon. The reason for this is obscure, unless the boy's own inclination is taken into account: the status of an apothecary surgeon in early Hanoverian times was very much below that of a doctor. William's uncle had been a Cambridge graduate, a respectable physician, yet here was William apprenticing his only son to a comparatively inglorious occupation: it was certainly not due to the father's lack of money, because when he came to make his will he could show a considerable amount. There is no record as to whom young William was apprenticed; if it was a local man, there seems to have been the choice of at least two—Mr. Thomas Hall,[30] or more probably, a Mr. Rock, who flourished in the neighbourhood about this time[31] and who was apothecary and surgeon to the local Overseers,[32] which was a post taken over by William himself in later years when he had finished his training. From the quality of his education and his ability to inoculate, it is

[23] Wors. Par. Reg.

[24] In 1731 William acted as trustee under the will of Robt. Hall, who called himself brother-in-law, ignoring the step-relationship. (Will dated 19 Mar. 1730, proved 1 Nov. 1731). Again in 1735 he was trustee under the will of his mother-in-law, who left him £100 and the children £5 each. (Elmhirst MSS.)

[25] 1718 and 1720. *Hist. Wors.*, p. 313.

[26] Bapt. 14 July 1726. Wors. Par. Reg.

[27] The Earl of Strafford had obtained the Manor rights about 1705, hitherto they had naturally belonged to the owner of Worsbrough Hall. (*Hist. Wors.*, p. 438.)

[28] Worsbrough Court Baron held 11 Nov. 1737. (Elmhirst MS.)

[29] Buried Worsbrough, 25 March 1740. Par. Reg.

[30] Buried Worsbrough, 28 Jan. 1748. Par. Reg.

[31] Parish Records, 1718-37. (*Hist. Wors.*, p. 367.)

[32] Worsbrough Workhouse was founded in 1737. (*Hist. Wors.*, p. 357.)

possible that the boy studied under one of the pioneers of inoculation such as Nettleton of Halifax, who had a great reputation in the north of England at this period. The terms of a surgical apprenticeship were strict and sanctioned by time: the young man was committed for five years, he had to serve faithfully his master and to promise that he would "not at any time obliterate, spoil, destroy, waste, embezzle, spend, or make away with any of the books, papers, prescriptions, monies or other property" of his master. More positively, he had to promise to "readily and chearfully obey and execute lawful and reasonable commands and shall not absent himself without leave, always conducting himself with all due diligence, honesty, sobriety and temperance."[33] The cost of such an apprenticeship was usually between £200 and £500 at this time, according to the fame of the master, who, in return for this sum, promised education, board and lodging.

Having arranged for his son's training, William senior made his will; in this document he called himself William Elmhirst of Ouslethwaite, Gentleman, suggesting that he no longer lived in Genn House, but had been leased the old building of which part still remains embedded in the present Ouslethwaite.[34] The will itself was a simple document as befitted a gentleman farmer with but one son. After the routine request to be buried in the north alley of Worsbrough Church, he gave all his lands in Worsbroughdale to young William. The unmarried daughters were to get £220 apiece and he added that the two girls, "may continue in Oyslethwaite, if I should die before my son William be loose of his apprenticeship, that is the twenty-fourth day of June next [1743], rent free. The married daughter, Sarah, did not do so well: her husband had borrowed £200 from old William, who now merely released him from his debt.[35]

Just as Dr. William had paid sixteen guineas towards the forces raised to repel the barbarian Scot in 1715, so now, in the newer and more serious rebellion of the Young Pretender in 1745, another subscription had to be made, in the baroque language of the period:

> "to raise forces in opposition to a rebellion begun in Scotland, in favour of a Popish pretender, to support the Crown and dignity of his gracious Majesty King George, to maintain our lives and fortunes, our religion, our all, against arbitrary power and tyranny, against Popish idolatry and worse than Turkish barbarity, by fire and faggot, by bloody massacres and savage superstitions."

Thus was the document headed. William's contribution, as proprietor of Genn House, was listed at two guineas[36] which, the alternatives being considered, does not seem excessive.

---

[33] Extracted from terms of apprenticeship of Richd. Elmhirst with surgeon Chorley of Leeds, 1821, which is typical of all similar arrangements in the preceding century.

[34] Thos. Archdale was taxed as owner of Ouslethwaite in 1715 and 1745 (*Hist. Wors.*, pp. 16 and 27); and Alice, widow of Richd. Archdale, sold the place to Mr. Hammersley, of Doncaster, 16 June 1748. (Elmhirst MSS.)

[35] Will dated 5 July 1742. (Elmhirst MS.)

[36] *Hist. Wors.*, p. 27.

Four years after making his first will, sensing the approach of death and knowing that his riches had increased, he added a codicil by which his two still unmarried daughters were each to have a total of £250.[37] William died about a fortnight later and was buried, as he had asked to be, among his fathers.[38]

[37] Codicil dated 7 April 1746. (Elmhirst MS.)
[38] Buried Worsbrough, 24 April 1746. Wors. Par. Reg.

GENERATION XII

WILLIAM ELMHIRST, THE SURGEON APOTHECARY
OF GENN HOUSE AND ELMHIRST
1721-1773

When his father, the man whose ship had never reached home, died, the next William was about twenty-five years of age. Apart from the cousins living remotely in Lincolnshire his only other relatives were his three sisters. Sarah, the eldest and five years older than he, married to Robert Greaves, still lived at Clayton Hall. The next sister, Anne, was twenty-seven and was to marry John Cawood of Rob Royd nearby. Youngest of all was Martha, who was twenty when their father died and who was destined to die unmarried.

William's apprenticeship, which his father had considered when making his will, ended in the summer of 1743[1] and William the elder did not die for another three years afterwards;[2] then, in the October following, young William, newly-qualified, was admitted to the ancestral copyhold estates[3] "on the death of his father William Elmhirst Gentleman." For more than a quarter of a century he was to live and work in the neighbourhood of Worsbroughdale. At the beginning he had many rivals, well-established men who rode their horses with heavy distinction and talked bad Latin with bland confidence. Later, as William grew older and more trusted, his practice enlarged, he was appointed surgeon-apothecary to the Workhouse, local gentry came to patronise him and he in turn took apprentices to try and make them into capable chemists and clinicians.

Throughout the greater part of his career William lived at Genn House or, as he wrote it, the house in Guen Lane, which in addition to the traditional advantages of a medical establishment being placed at cross-roads already had the proper atmosphere imparted to it by having been built and lived in by his great-uncle the physician. His sister Martha may have remained at the small house at Ouslethwaite where they had both been born, but she probably moved the few hundred yards to Genn House to help him as housekeeper, receptionist and nurse.

William seems to have filled his role as amateur farmer with responsibility untempered with enthusiasm. For the years for which records remain it is possible to calculate very exactly his farm livestock.[4] A system of Small Tithes, or rather local taxes in the place of those tithes, was employed in Worsbrough. For each sheep wintered the payment was a penny a head, for each lamb born

---

[1] 24 June 1743.
[2] Buried 24 April 1746. Wors. Par. Reg.
[3] 17 Oct. 1746.
[4] Reverse side of his Medical Ledger.

in the township twopence had to be paid with reductions for larger numbers than five. A pig that farrowed cost a shilling, a breeding goose sixpence, new-born foals and swarming bees shared the same rate of a penny. William regularly kept three cows, and his sheep averaged about fifty head. "Beese" swarmed erratically and there is only one record of a mare foaling.[5] He had an income of some £20 a year from selling his wheat and other crops; there were occasional windfalls such as the selling of fat oxen to Ellis the Barnsley butcher for about £10 apiece. His sheep, when he had them to sell, fetched just under £1 and lambs averaged seven shillings.

Another source of income, additional to that coming from his professional work, his farming activities at Genn House and Ouslethwaite and the rent of £30 from the tenant at Elmhirst,[6] was from the sale of the coal lying under his copyhold lands. By this time coal-collecting was becoming a more serious business than the mere superficial quarrying which had been scratching at the surface of the dale during the preceding five centuries; it was also becoming a more lethal occupation, in April 1765 John Tattershall was buried in Worsbrough churchyard "a Collier, killed in Mr. Elmhirst's pit." For a year's output of coal (1768 or 1769) William was paid £3 10s. 0d.[7] but this was probably less than he usually derived from this source.

All these incomes were of slight importance to the surgeon-apothecary compared with his professional emoluments. By accident the last of his medical account books has survived to the present day;[8] it is a thick, tall, narrow ledger in which he recorded the names of all his patients, their addresses and the various drugs and treatments that he supplied together with the charges that he made. It is impossible not to be impressed by these day-to-day notes, extracts from which follow, that so well reveal the man and his methods. This was no conscienceless quack whose prescriptions had given place to fewer and fewer shades of coloured water; to the end of his life treatments and medicines were the best that he had been taught in his apprenticeship. It would have been so understandably easy for him in that time and place to keep his clients satisfied with stock mixtures and pills named numerically. His local fame as an apothecary must have been considerable; physicians, then the loftiest form of medical life, used to send their patients to him with prescriptions that were to be dispensed. The greater part of William's business was in the sale of purges which were usually administered in the form of powders; these popular powders, adult size, regularly cost sixpence, for children the dose and price depended on age.

---

[5] His mares were called "Flower" and "Jewel". *Ibid.*

[6] Francis Hill, a patient of William's and a constipated tallow-chandler, was leased Elmhirst for 14 years from 1770. Deed of lease dated 7 April 1770. (Elmhirst MSS.)

[7] Account Books, Worsbrough Old Town, 1768/9. *Hist. Wors.*, p. 249.

[8] William's careful son could not bear to see so many empty pages wasted and, having filled it with his own meticulous notes, was still less inclined to throw it away.

" 5th Apl. 1769.   Mr. Hall; Blackmore.
    Pul. iij purg.   [3 purgative powders]
        Mr. Geo.   1.4
        Eodem Miss Tetty   1.4
        Eodem Miss Salley   1.4
        Eodem Miss Fanney   1.2
        Eodem Miss Knelly   1.2

30th Jan. 1769.   John Oxley; Barnsley.
    Pulv. Purg.   ˙ Eldest [child]
        Do.   secundo
        Do.   youngest
    these are not to be charged, they were given. "

Whole families purged themselves at the same time, man, wife and brood of children; nowadays this might seem to be a foolhardy arrangement, but then many houses, Ouslethwaite among them, had privies which could accommodate several members of the household side by side in uninhibited juxtaposition.

Another powder in great demand was the Antiscorbutic: these were popular all round the calendar, not particularly so in the winter and early spring months, when scurvy would have been most common.   Asthmatic mixtures, electuaries, carminative mixtures and a variety of cordials supplied a lot of business.   Other treatments were more ambitious, syphilitics started with a frankly-named Pox Lotion and thereafter graduated to gobbets of mercurial ointment to rub into themselves:

" 15 May 1768.   Mr. P. . . .
        Lotio Poxe. ·
    29 May.   Ungt. Merc. "

A peculiar treatment was an emplastrum for a rupture: it would seem that this was employed only in cases where a hernia had become either irreducible or strangulated; the amazing thing is that some of these patients survived.   One fortunate man at least lived along enough to reappear in the ledger after a considerable interval.

As regards the surgical side to his profession, distinct from his duties as apothecary, William had three main occupations—blood-letting, inoculations and operative surgery.

Very frequently he was called in to bleed the plethoric countrymen of Hanoverian Yorkshire.   This was a fearsome procedure by modern standards: in his waistcoat or greatcoat pocket William would have carried a single folding lancet or a couple of more elegant knives in a silver case.   The short blade was extracted and any redundant pocket fluff removed from it while the patient rolled up his sleeve.   A bowl having been put in position under the extended arm, the vein was incised and as much blood was allowed to flow as was considered to be appropriate, for most men this was usually a pint or half a pint, then

the arm was bandaged and the bleeding stopped.   For such venesections, the
standard charge was a shilling:

```
" Wm. Rhodes Jr.   Ward Green.
      7 June 1768.
            Mixt. Salini              1.10
            Vena sectio               Nil
      Francis Edmunds Esq.
        5 Sept. 1768.
                V.S. et itinere meo.  1.0
      Mr. Parkin.  Mortomley.
        12 Oct. 1768.
                Phlebotomia.  Mrs⁹   1.0 "
```

It is in the matter of smallpox inoculations that William was of the greatest
service to his time and generation.   Smallpox was then endemic throughout
the world; very commonly it was fatal[10]; those who survived were left with faces
pitted and scarred.   Children were especially liable to the infection; contemporary advertisement by nurses, wet or dry, seeking employment, specified
that the girl was "Well marked with the Small Pox" and therefore not liable to
convey the disease to her charges.   In an attempt to lessen the severity of the
disease, then considered almost inevitable, inoculation was introduced.   The
surgeon to the British Embassy in Adrianople learnt the technique from an old
Greek woman there; returning to England, he did the first such inoculation
here in the year 1721.   The practice was considered dangerous.   He gave a
demonstration series of inoculations on six felons in Newgate, all of these
survived and were subsequently pardoned.   Later, as was certain to happen,
misadventures and deaths were reported and inoculation fell into disfavour.
Dr. Wagstaffe, Physician to St. Batholomew's Hospital, considered that:

> "posterity would marvel that a practice employed by a few ignorant women amongst an
> illiterate and unthinking people, should have so suddenly been adopted by one of the
> politest nations in the world."

By 1729 less than forty inoculations were done in the course of the year,
of these no less than three had died.   During the years that William was an
apprentice it remained an exceptionable procedure and it is surprising that he
ever had the opportunity to learn the technique.   Later the great Dr. Mead
declared himself in favour and, as with childbirth anaesthetics a century later,
a royal example was set.   The Princess of Wales had her children inoculated in
1754, after it had been given a preliminary test on some charity children,
thoughtfully chosen to take the place of adult criminals.[11]

The method of inoculation was simple and different from the modern

---

[9] This is an exception to the general rule that women were not bled.   It was considered that nature coped
satisfactorily on its own.
[10] Worsbrough Parish Register records the burial of two sisters, "both dead from the Small pox", on
8 July 1763.
[11] Edgar Crookshank: *History of Vaccination.*   London, 1889.

technique of vaccination with cow-pox. A patient who already had smallpox in a mild form acted as donor, pus from a "fresh and kindly Pock" was collected from this individual and scratched with a lancet into the arm of the child.[12] The area was then protected with an inverted walnut shell covered with an adhesive dressing. Once the arm showed signs of reaction it was dressed with warm cabbage leaves. The dangers were obvious, the child was given nothing less than smallpox and this was itself occasionally fatal; more usually the child was not dangerously ill and the face emerged comparatively unscarred. Perhaps it was because of this element of chance that the apothecary surgeon made no regular charge for inoculation; it was mentioned in the bill together with any journeys made and the whole priced at "what you please":

"4 Jan. 1770. Francis Edmunds Esq. Delivered all the above Bills to Mr. Edmunds wch. makes in all when cast up together £171 11s. 6d. For inoculating Master and Miss Gower and for applications used to Little Miss Gower's Breast, Riding Charges and Attendance dureinge the time I've been Employed what you please.

"24 Mar. 1769. Mr. Hall, Blackmore. Itinere meo pro inoculating 5 children [no charge].

"2 Apl. 1769. John Hurst, Howhouse. For Plaisters salves used to yr. child and for inoculating her what you please."

Apart from bloodletting and inoculations there was the occasional tooth that was brought to William for extraction: this was rarely done save for friends and acquaintances, such as the Edmunds living at Worsbrough Hall; most people kept their troublesome teeth to themselves or waited for the itinerant tooth-drawer at Barnsley Fair or elsewhere:

"18 Mch. 1770. Francis Edmunds Esq.
Pro Dente attrahente   3.0
Liniment hemorrhoid   0.6"

Properly surgical in the modern sense were the treatments for injuries, for cuts and bruises, dislocations and fractures. For wounds, William had a tincture which was probably not very effective, certainly it was not applied for the object of keeping the wound clean; infection and pus were expected with every large wound and according to colour, consistency and stench, the pus was "laudable" or otherwise.

Dislocations seem to have been satisfactorily reduced. Among his patients he had a repeated source of income in a dislocated jaw, which, then as now, tended to redislocate at irregular intervals. Fractures were almost as inactively treated as wounds. The routine was to reduce the broken bone by pulling it approximately into line, when it no longer offended aesthetically it was left to heal itself as best it could in its corrected position between splints. Once

---

[12] When William's great-great-grandson was an infant, the same primitive method was still in use on the Continent. "As to the child's being vaccinated," wrote its father, "I am anxious for it to be done, but the difficulty is to find a child whose parents are healthy. In a large manufacturing town like Lyons, most of the men have something the matter with them, and consequently their offspring are anything but sound. Absinthe and debauchery have wrought much evil amongst the artisan class. If you can get some matter from a really healthy infant, have the boy vaccinated." Henry Elmhirst-Baxter, M.R.C.S., to his wife, 23 Sept. 1882.

thus straightened, William lost interest in his fractures and he rarely seemed to revisit such cases later:

> "9 Nov. 1768. John Copley.
> Pro reducing a Dislocated
> Elbow [of] Apprentice   7.6
> 28 Oct. 1770. Josh. Shay.
> for Redg. fractured leg and
> applications thereto   £1.10.0
> 10 June 1770. Fr. Edmunds Esq.
> pro cureing yr. servt. Tom's
> leg when bit by Dog   £1.10.0"

More dramatic than injuries and dislocations, were the occasional small amputation:

> "28 Feb. 1769. Mr. Wood.
> Pro amputat. tuum Index   £1.1.0"

Because so much of the record is missing there are notes on only one major operation; this concerned the removal of a leg on 28 May 1770. The patient was Thomas Gelder, a poor old inhabitant of the Workhouse in Worsbrough, but the bill for three guineas was settled by the Overseers. The operation was no sudden decision, for a long while previously William had been temporising and treating the leg, doubtless a senile gangrene, with local applications in the hope that the trouble would settle itself. Three weeks after his last visit, the operation could be postponed no longer. Probably the Workhouse Overseers were in attendance to give official tone to the whole affair; perhaps some of the inmates helped hold poor Thomas down while the slashing and sawing went on. The old man survived; years later he was swallowing tablets, still resident in the workhouse. It is perhaps not so surprising that William should have been lucky in this patient when so many expert surgeons in famous hospitals more usually had fatal results after their removals of limbs; the cause was doubtless that the hospitals and their straw mattresses smouldered with the bacteria of St. Anthony's Fire, while the Worsbrough Workhouse, depressing though it may have been, was probably bacteriologically more select.

Added to all these responsibilities as gentleman farmer, apothecary and surgeon, William also had a small veterinary practice. His most popular animal medicine was a horse drench, constituents unrecorded, in great demand at the considerable cost of one and ninepence. Occasionally he even dispensed for the dogs for whom his Latin was not unsuited:

> "17 Sept. 1768. Francis Edmunds Esq.
> Pro curante Abscess sub
> ejus Brachio Godfrey   £1.1.0
> Ungt. Merc. olea pro canibus 1.0
> 1772. Mr. Cawood.
> A drench pro equam.   1.9"

William lived a bachelor at Genn House for close on fifteen years. But on 20 October 1757 he was married in Worsbrough Church by the Vicar of Ecclesfield to Elizabeth, the daughter of John Wordsworth, of Tankersley.[13] He was nearly twice the age of his nineteen-year-old wife. Children arrived at intervals, well spaced for those days; a son, William, in 1759, a daughter, Elizabeth, two years later, and another son, Thomas, after a further two years. Thomas died a few days later. In two more years a last child, Martha, was born. The children were educated locally. Mr. Samuel Chaddick did some part-time tutoring and more thorough foundations were laid by the local parson, Mr. Jeremiah Dixon, who fortunately was as interested in his own digestive processes as are most clerics, a fact that enabled William to set the cost of the children's schooling against the medicines swallowed by their usher. The library, which had been left to the school in Worsbrough by Obadiah Walker, was fully employed to supplement more active teaching. Most of these volumes were concerned with church heresies of the first few Christian eras (in Latin) and the farmers' children must have had their minds considerably broadened.

Only the fourth and last of the surgeon apothecary's ledgers has survived. The accounts begin in May 1768 with many references to the preceding volume III, entries thereafter are continuous until the time of his death in 1773. He usually made all the entries himself, but occasionally the current apprentice made an addition. By means of this book a very reasonable estimate can be made of the size of William's practice. As might have been anticipated, February was the busiest month; then were the country people most cold and miserable, for months they had been living on salted meat and root vegetables, often crowded together for warmth in insanitary hovels. In February 1769, for instance, William had eight-six patients, a number not large in itself, but which in those days repre-sented a considerable amount of work, because only the nearby few would send to Genn House for a bottle of medicine, or go there to attend the surgery. Many would send a message by somebody passing nearby and William would be expected to ride down the muddy lanes on the back of one of his mares. For the actual journey William never made a charge; it was often entered at the foot of the bill as "Itinere meo. What you will", or occasionally a more impressive: "Riding charges and Attendance what you please."

An average month of professional work brought an income of some £30, from this must be deducted the cost of the drugs, leaving him an income of some £250 a year, a considerable amount; for his farm produce and coal he probably got almost another £50. The degree of his material prosperity can be gauged

---

[13] Details are thus recorded in the Parish Register which must be presumed to be correct. But in the published Wordsworth pedigrees there is no Elizabeth among the three daughters of John Wordsworth of Hermit Hill, near Tankersley; on the other hand, there was a John Wordsworth, of Penistone, a mercer who lived 1703-1770, who had an only daughter Elizabeth, who was baptised there 9 March 1738. This was the year that Elizabeth Elmhirst née Wordsworth, was born. (Gordon Wordsworth: *Notes on the Wordsworths of Penistone*. 4to. 1929. E. J. Bedford: *Genealogical Memoranda on Family of Wordsworth*. 4to. 1881.)

by the fact that in 1768 he bought the rest of Ouslethwaite from Thomas Hammersley for £3,000; this property was auctioned at the White Bear[14] in Barnsley on the afternoon of Monday, 12 December. In the manuscript notice of sale is the comment: "It is to be observed that Mr. Elmhirst hath for sevl. Years last past paid £20 per Annum for the use of a Sough[15] but he now not using his Collierys adjoining thereto hath lately discontinued the payment thereof." The sale was to open with a bid of £3,000 with advances of not less than £40: "A Watch shall be set upon the Table and when the Hour Hand points at 6 O'Clock the then last Bidder shall be the purchaser." It follows therefore that nobody bid against William: the deeds of the property were handed over to him in August 1769. His object was plainly either to invest his capital securely, since he was quite uninterested in farming, or else to build there a big house for himself; the last alternative is the more probable because since Houndhill had been lost to the family their headquarters had been Genn House, never an imposing residence, and the small house on part of Ouslethwaite.

William never expected to get all his bills paid in cash; a hard core of them, though by no means as large a percentage as to-day, was never paid at all. A great many others were settled by barter or services, such an arrangement well suited both parties to the bargain; a chimney-piece wanted mending, a steer was wanted for the farm, a side of pig for the larder, or perhaps a couple of fields needed hedging: all were accepted in return for professional services:

"2nd May 1770. Thos. Wells, Barnsley.
For professional services 3.11

Nov. 22. Recd. Fish .6
Dec. 2. Fish and Cockles .7
Dec. 23. Cockles .5
Jan. 1 1773. Fish .7
Remains due 1.10"

"28 Oct. 1770. Josh. Shay.
For Redg. fractured leg and
applications thereto £1.10.0
For applications &c. used to
your Daughter's Arm . £1.1.0
Total. Various Drugs £3.2.6

Recd. in pt. of ye above £2.0.0
Recd. 3 Sheep £1.2.0
Due to Ballance · £0.0.6"

By 1773, the year the ledger ends, William was busy and prosperous. Two years before, after Mr. Glanvile the surgeon apothecary had died at Rob Royd and was buried at Worsbrough,[16] his practice had correspondingly increased.

---

[14] Later renamed The Royal Hotel. (Hist. Wors., p. 159.)
[15] Probably a movable covering for attacking a coal face.
[16] 25 April 1771. Hist. Wors., p. 341.

He was now employing his fifth apprentice, a youth called John Hayes.[17] His son, a serious studious thirteen years of age, had outgrown what the local parson taught and was sent to school with a Mr. Whitley.[18]

In the summer William must have had a pleasant job for an unambitious man; jogging quietly on his old mare to Stainborough, Wombwell or Oughtibridge, and wherever his patients and friends might be; gossiping contentedly on the state of the harvest, trying to avoid being drawn on to the topic of his patients' illnesses. In the winter there was little pleasure to be had. Cold blustering days, when the mare steamed and the saddle got wet, when the lanes disappeared into tracks of mud, and everyone had a sore throat. The dreadful roads were only then just being improved by the local authorities. A system of turnpikes was being set up, at each such place the traffic was halted and all travellers had to pay towards the upkeep of the highways.

It was at one of these barriers, the Hangman-stone Toll Bar,[19] that the unexpected happened. William was probably calling on a patient nearby, a Richard Cooper, whom he had seen a little earlier. Perhaps the mare was startled by a new-painted toll bar, perhaps she shied at a sudden carriage. Whatever the cause, good, kind and worthy William was there thrown from his horse and straightway died.

---

[17] His first apprentice was called Rock, after him came a relation of William's called William Walker, and then two nephews, Richard and Robert Greaves. (Will of William Elmhirst dated 7 May 1767, and Robert Elmhirst's memorandum of 1830.)

[18] Fly-leaves of Medical Ledger.

[19] On the Sheffield road to the north side of Tankersley Common.

GENERATION XIII

WILLIAM ELMHIRST OF OUSLETHWAITE AND ELMHIRST
1759-1821

When the surgeon-apothecary so abruptly died, he left his young widow with a great many responsibilities. She was thirty-five; the boy was only fourteen and the two girls twelve and eight years old. Her husband was buried, as he had wished to be, with his ancestors in Worsbrough.[1] From the records of the executors' accounts, only three mourning rings seem to have been bought, costing a guinea apiece, for distribution.[2]

By his will he had left all the property to his son; the only provisos were that his widow should receive an annuity of £50 a year and that each of the girls should have £800, with interest, when she married or came of age.

Elizabeth for the time being controlled the Worsbrough properties in very much the same unadventurous spirit which had marked her late husband's agricultural methods. For a short while even the surgical and medical practice was continued by John Hayes, the last apprentice: after a few weeks, business dwindled and thereafter the youth helped her in the unpleasant taks of collecting all the bad debts in the medical ledgers; this she managed with some pertinacity and bills were sent out for sums which had been owing for many, many years. By chance, because the apprentice doodled on it, as he doodled on everything else (even the notice of the sale of Ouslethwaite is garnished with pigeons eating berries, cherub's and horses' heads); one such post-mortem bill has survived; this concerned medical services rendered as long ago as between 1759 and 1763, and is headed to the recipient as "Debtor to ye Executors of the late Wm. Elmhirst." In this manner she collected several hundred pounds.[3] Other debts were settled by instalments and others by various services and barters, as each account was closed she initialled or signed it in the ledger. At the same time, in November 1773, an advertisement appeared four times in the York Courant newspaper,[4] asking all who owed the dead man money to pay the same to his widow. Those who had claims against the estate were asked to send in their accounts. Meanwhile, Genn House was cleared of medical debris; the dusty shelves and stale stock were taken down and sold. Then the young widow bought a harpsichord to fight the gloom and emptiness of silent rooms.[5]

---

[1] Buried 19 July 1773 (Wors. Par. Reg.) in the aisle between the porch door and the north door. (William Elmhirst to Frederick Fisher, 4 Sept. 1838.)

[2] Executors' Accounts. Settled 27 Feb. 1783.

[3] Between 20 Aug. 1773 and 26 Oct. 1782. £348 was thus collected. (Executors' Accounts.)

[4] Copy of the newspaper for 30 Nov. 1773 is in the York Minster Library.

[5] Executors' Accounts. Settled 27 Feb. 1783.

One of her first official functions as temporary head of the family was to appear in the Manor Court, together with the other trustees, to claim admittance to the copyhold lands of Elmhirst and Genn House.[6]

Perhaps she had seen enough of doctoring; she knew all about the irregular hours, meals growing cold or getting burnt, dirty dressings lying about the surgery, mud trampled into the house by a succession of patients. It was decided that young Willy should become a lawyer, and soon after his seventeenth birthday a premium of £150 was paid to have him articled to Mr. West, of Cawthorne.[7] As a fellow clerk and pupil there, he found George Wood, from Monk Bretton. The training they received was excellent. George subsequently became a famous judge.[8] Little Willy,[9] uninspired and methodical, learned all the intricacies of efficient book-keeping. From West's William graduated to Mr. Allen's in Furnivals Inn, in London; he was still there in town at the age of twenty-three. In the spring of that year he signed himself "of ffurnivalls Inn"[10], but by November he was back in Worsbrough.[11] Allen always remained a close friend and adviser,[12] young William sent legal questions, money to invest, hams and game to Furnivals Inn; in return came the answers, occasional Counsel's opinion and a barrel or two of oysters. His legal activities were, however, always very limited.

For the next forty years William took the centre of the local stage. He was, as he wrote, an Attorney of His Majesty's Court of King's Bench at Westminster,[13] he was owner of Ouslethwaite,[14] copyholdowner of Elmhirst and Genn House.[15] More important than this, he was a good, humourless man, earnest and efficient to the end of his days.

The change in the control of affairs was soon apparent. The searcher among family papers is all at once overwhelmed by an excess of evidence. William made notes of everything. Every penny spent was recorded, sometimes entered three times in separate notebooks. Throughout a great part of his life he kept half-a-dozen different series of accounts, all filled from cover to cover in minute writing. Never in all these entries was there any suggestion of even momentary relaxation and only once, when overwhelmed by personal bereavement, did he give way sufficiently to record a feeling.

The books which now exist are in six series. For each year he had separate pocket account books[16]; a fat, thick pocket-book duplicated a great many of

[6] Court Roll; Saturday, 6 Nov. 1773.
[7] Account dated 30 Aug. 1776.
[8] Hist. Wors., p. 151.
[9] He weighed just over 9 stone. 3 Nov. 1780.
[10] Lease from Spencer Stanhope of lands in Silkstone to George Shirt. 12 Feb. 1782.
[11] Legal Notebook, letter to J. Allen. 13 Nov. 1784.
[12] In 1805 Allen retired, the firm became Allen, Exley & Stocker. (Letter from him of 25 July 1805.)
[13] Letter to Allen. 4 Nov. 1785.
[14] 60 acres in 1783 Assessment.
[15] Together 52 acres in 1783 Assessment.
[16] 1787-1821.

these[17]; incidental accounts were kept on loose bits of paper[18]; taxes and assessments filled another account[19]; there was a servants and wages account book[20]; and lastly there was the chief general account book into which a great many of the entries were copied from other sources.[21]

The year after his return into Yorkshire saw the marriage of his elder sister, Elizabeth, to Thomas Taylor, of Park House. It was socially a satisfactory but unexciting marriage; the bridegroom was more than twice as old as Elizabeth and they never had any children. Martha, the other sister, remained a spinster.

William was early an addict of local auctions. This first year of his independence he bought a peculiar assortment at a bankrupt's sale, a fishing-rod but a print of "The Devout Family". Later the same year he bought a cane with a sword in it which still survives, and, together with a collection of law books, complete sets of English and Roman histories and the inevitable Plutarch's "Lives".

Many of the other purchases in the early days and indeed throughout the rest of his life, were of horses. He bought shrewdly and bred some fine animals. The life history of every horse was discoverable from one or more of the notebooks, when it was foaled, when it was first ridden, when each shoe was put on, when it was sold, or when it died. The mating of his mares became more and more of a serious business towards the latter part of his life. He kept the handbills advertising various stallions and their pedigrees; where pedigrees were incomplete, he wrote to former owners and made further enquiries. All costs, including the tips paid to ostlers and grooms, are recorded. Throughout his life he hunted, but the sport was never allowed to become an obsession or to interfere with his primary duty as an estate manager. The first purchases for his stable were made through Taylor, his newly acquired brother-in-law. There is no record of any of his animals racing, which is odd because he would have had no moral objection; packs of cards, for instance, those other playthings of the Devil, were always being purchased. William had probably seen enough estates ruined by absentee hunting squires and was determined to avoid that error.

Other livestock was bought equally carefully. His dead father's flock, forty sheep, was soon reinforced and replaced by woollier, fatter creatures sired by rams of known performance. Breeding was carefully controlled; no haphazard natural processes for William; ewes served by one ram were marked on the left ear, by another ram the mark was on the right ear, by yet another the mark was at the bottom of both ears. His cows were no less carefully matched, good bulls were hired and brought considerable distances to better the stock.

---

[17] 1803-1821.
[18] 1800-1804.
[19] 1783-1821.
[20] 1783-1806.
[21] 1783-1806.

It was men such as William who had revolutionised agriculture in England by the close of the century.

These were typical entries of the early days:

"1784. Nov. 3. Paid John Hammerton, Smithley, for a brinded Bull then about 2 years old (he abated 3s. viz., 2s. 6d. by Agreement and 6d. for luck).

1785. Jan. 10. Paid Thos. Taylor Esq., for a dun Mare called 'Bounce' that will be five years old next Spring. £12.12.0.

1785. Apr. 23. Sunday school. Paid into the hands of Mr. Jas. Sykes to be by him transmitted to Mrs. Edmunds as my subscription. £2.2.0.

[This subscription was paid yearly hereafter.]

1785. May 16. Paid Edm. Parkin for his son driving the plow 20 days at 2d. 3s. 4d.

1785. June 24. Paid Mother as under. For Girls [servants at Genn House] wages due Martinmas 1784, £6. For a year and half's Annuity due Lady Day, 1785, £75. On account of sister Martha's Interest of her Fortune, £7.12.9."[22]

The best paid of William's farm servants, George Hirst, the farm manager, was being paid at this period at the annual rate of £14.

In 1785 there began the first of a whole series of new forms of taxation designed to pay for the disastrous struggle with the American colonies and the perpetual French wars. In the beginning the sums were relatively small:

"1785. Dec. 22. Paid new Window Duty	£1.0.0.
3/4 Year's Tax on a Male Servant	£1.17.6.
Do. on a Female	3.9.
1/2 Year's Tax on 2 Saddle Horses	10.0.
Do. on a Waggon	4.0."

All these were luxury taxes, farm employees and farm horses escaped taxation; the waggon was the vehicle by which the women of the family travelled, not to be confused with those used on the farms. In addition to the new taxes, there were local rates to pay; the toll-gate charges had proved insufficient to maintain the new roadways. Then there was the Poor Assessment and the charge towards the payment of the local constable.

Alcoholic drinks by being locally brewed did not thus escape taxation. William usually gave his own grain to a professional brewer, who was responsible for the payment of excise:

"1786. Feb. 17. Paid Mr. Jonathan West for 21 Gallons of Red Port at 7s. 9d. Gallon. £8.3.7.

For making 8 Quarters of Barley into malted in January 1786, Excise 10s. 6d. and wages 2s. 6d.

1786. Mar. 25. Paid Mr. Greaves what he paid Messrs. Brooke of Leeds for 12 Gallons (at 7s. 6d. a Gallon) of Calcavilla Wine and for the Bottles containing the same Wine. £5.3.0.

1786. Dec. 6. Received of Revd. Mr. Lodge for bay Mare sold in April 1786 [bought at Barnsley Fair, 10th October 1783] £14, and for his sheep being in High Field at

---

[22] These and all similar subsequent dated entries, unless otherwise stated, are taken from the General Accounts Book.

Turnips in 1786, 14s. Returned him 2 Guineas on account of the Mare's eyes proving bad.''

In the matter of the bay mare's eyes, William seems to have been rather too smart. He had had the mare for more than two years and it would be very surprising if so astute a horse-dealer had not discovered about the eyes previously. Perhaps he was waiting to see whether the parson would find it out, too, and when he did so, William's undoubted virtue prevailed and the two guineas were returned with appropriate apologies.

In other ways he was not so shrewd. A couple of months previously he had sent a most ingenuous enquiry to his old friend and adviser, Mr. Allen of Furnivals Inn. He only faintly disguised himself:

"A person of 27 or 28 years of Age in Possession of £300 is informed that by sinking that sum in a Fund in London and receiving no Benefit for 7, 8 or some such No. of years he may afterwards receive an Annuity of £100 for his Life, be pleased to inform me whether such proceedings be practicable and if so what are the steps necessary to be taken for sinking his Money.''[23]

The London lawyer's answer had not survived. More certain than the London fund, William's farming methods and efficiency were already paying dividends. Meanwhile, the death of a remote relation, his father's second cousin, old, childless Mordecai Cutts,[24] brought him hundreds of acres lying clustered at Thorne, Fishlake, Sykehouse and Wroot, some twenty-five miles to the east of Worsbrough. In Thorne Church he caused a monument to be erected to his benefactor[25]; it still remains there on the north side of the chancel, Mordecai in a large formal wig facing in one direction, a greyhound's head, his crest, facing in another, all tastefully and not too expensively decorated in the classical style.

Now, too, William decided to start the building of a bigger and better house more worthy of squiredom. His home at Ouslethwaite was small, Genn House, though only about a century old, was rambling and unimpressive. His new house, the foundations of which were now laid, was to replace the older building at Ouslethwaite. Local labour was employed.[26]

"1788. Sept. 23. Paid William Banker for making 68,840 Clap't Bricks at 10s. and 2,000 Common ones at 6s. 9d. per thousand. £35.1.0.

1788. Sept. 23. Paid Francis Downing of Wiremills for an English Setting Dog. £2.2.0.''

William's legal practice, never extensive, was now almost finished; he found all his available time was being taken by farming and local affairs. One of his last letters on legal matters to Furnivals Inn reads:

[23] Legal Notebook. Letter dated 12 Oct. 1786.
[24] 1787. See Appendix H.
[25] Letter from Wm. Middlebrook to Wm. Elmhirst, 14 July 1791.
[26] The chief carpenter, Joshua Watson and his wife "were both, long before they died, kept by the Parish of Worsbrough.'' Evidence of Lawrence Dyer. April 1831.

"Jonathon Firth agt. Eliz. Hatfield, widow.

The Deft. left the country before she could be arrested and I was yesterday informed she and daughter live at No. 7, New Square, Minories, London, therefore inclose the Bond whereon the Action is brought and beg you'll take out Ab. and endeavour to have her arrested. Mrs. Hatfield and her daughter are Flowerers or Workers of Waistcoats and Handkerchiefs and I'm told the Officer is most likely to gain Admittance to the Defendant by applying to have something worked. She is apprised of the Suit being commenced and am apprehensive will not be taken unless some Deception be used."[27]

Little did William know, nor would he have greatly cared, that the age of Waistcoat Flowerers was doomed, that very summer the Bastille was to fall.

His own clothing was simple and useful. He bought pair after pair of leathern breeches, which cost him 27 shillings, every three months. His waistcoats were plain, coats and topcoats were all serviceable and little else.

"1789. Sept. 4. Paid Mr. John Drake for a Coat. £2.10.7½d.
1790. Jul. 2. Paid Earnshaw & Royston for a Top Coat. £2.7.0."

Tidy and methodical in everything, he now arranged to have a suitable wife. He became engaged to his second cousin, Ann Rachel Elmhirst, the only child and heiress of Captain Thomas Elmhirst, of Stixwould Abbey in Lincolnshire.[28] Not only was she destined to inherit her father's property at Stixwould, but she would also inherit more lands from her mother, who held in trust for her many acres in Brigsley, East Halton and Worlaby, in Lincolnshire.[29]

A marriage settlement was composed, a complicated document by which she was to bring with her as her marriage portion the sum of £4,000. William in return made over various properties to his future father-in-law in trust for Ann Rachel. From these properties he reserved the coal rights, growing yearly more valuable, to himself.[30] The settlement agreed upon, William sealed it with a new seal of his arms,[31] to which the crest of a hurst of elms had now been added. Thomas of Stixwould, however, used on the same document a fine baroque seal, made when he was young, showing the arms that had been used in 1657.

William was thirty-one; Ann Rachel only twenty at this time. Ouslethwaite was in chaos, frantic carpenters hammering, the reek of wet paint, odd nails, sawdust and wood-shavings on the floor, doors that would not shut, and windows that would not open. Furthermore, the place still had to be appropriately furnished:

"1790. Oct. 13. Paid Mr. Thomas Hall for 24 yards of lush cloth for 2 pairs sheets at 2s. 8d. £3.4.0."

Three days after the marriage settlement had been signed, William and Ann Rachel were married at Stixwould. The bride proved to be a fierce, busy,

---

[27] Letter to Messrs. Allen dated 8 May 1789.
[28] See Appendices E, F and G for exact relationship.
[29] Will of Ann's grandfather, Theophilus Smith, dated 11 March 1783.
[30] Marriage Settlement dated 6 Nov. 1790.
[31] With the plain canton sable. As claimed in 1665.

dominating little woman, a great deal of whose youth seems to have been employed in composing moral platitudes, which she then wrote out carefully inside printed or penned frames. A sheaf of these survives, one example will be sufficient:

> "Learn to live well, that you mayst die so too:
> To live and die is all we have to do."

William's mother, the surgeon's widow, had wisely decided to stop at Genn House, away from the young couple. Here she lived the rest of her life with her spaniel and her harpsichord, only a short way from the new hall.

All William's expenses, even though a great many bills had not yet been sent in, had involved him in a lot of spending. To raise money he decided to lease out both Elmhirst and the now unwanted farmlands related to Genn House. The serf's shackles, though light as gossamer, were still around his ankles. The Lord of the Manor pounced upon him because the leases had been arranged without the lord's licence and contrary to the custom of the manor. As was most certainly his right, the Lord of the Manor, now the same Earl of Strafford who used to give William his subscriptions to be paid to the York Assembly Rooms and the Races, said that by this lease William had forfeited his right to the copyhold lands. At weekly intervals thereafter the Manor Court heard a token query made as to whether anyone would come forward to claim the properties. It was all made the more theatrical because at that time William himself was acting as the Steward of the Court.[32] The third and last query was made on 27 December 1790. William then came forward, confessed his error, paid himself the fine of a year's rent and was once again admitted copyhold tenant. One is tempted to believe the whole of this ritual was bogus; it is difficult to imagine the efficient steward-lawyer making such a false step. Some previous arrangement may have been made with Strafford whereby the wrong should be admitted, a token fine paid and the tenants at Elmhirst and Genn should continue to pay rent to William. There is certainly nothing documentary to show they were evicted from either property.

The bills engendered by the wedding crowded for payment:

"1790. Dec. 16. Paid Mr. John Noble for Repairing Chaise. £5.4.8.
1790. Dec. 17. Paid Mr. Vickers for Painting Chaise. £6.6.0.
1790. Dec. 17. Paid Earnshaw & Royston for Tornalet Waistcoat and Requisites, 11s. 9d.
1790. Dec. 18. Paid Mr. Darbyshire for Silver Plate. £38.3.7."

The first year of married life saw a great many changes in the way of life of William of Ouslethwaite. Ann Rachel and her formidable determination were probably responsible. The single male servant was now reinforced by a second, the number of saddle horses was increased to four, one of which was for the use of the widow at Genn House, and the new chaise ousted the more homely waggon

---

[32] He succeeded Richard Fenton in 1789 and was succeeded by Birks in 1800. (*Hist. Wors.*, p. 439.)

in which earlier Elmhirsts had travelled. The difference in luxury may be seen by the increased rate of taxation; the trundling waggon used only to cost an annual eight shillings, but the brisk new carriage was costing £16 yearly.[33] Ann Rachel made short journeys in her black Sedan Chair which is still in existence in Darfield.

During the same period William's father-in-law, the militia Captain from Stixwould Abbey, moved out of Lincolnshire and came to live at Swaith House, a couple of miles east of Ouslethwaite. William dealt with a lot of his affairs and managed for him his rates and local taxes.

The metamorphosis continued:

> "1791. Paid Mr. Thos. Hall, 2 Handkerchiefs 4s. 4d.,
> 2¾ Yards Cambric for Rufflesat 12s. £2.2.0."

About a year after the wedding the first child was born,[34] a son, inevitably called William. For the christening there was more finery:

> "1791. Dec. 2. Paid Mr. Earnshaw for a Coat. £2.4.10½.
> 1791. Dec 2. Paid Mr. Drake for a kind of Kersemere to make a Waistcoat, 11s. 9d., with something for celebrations.
> 1792. Jan. 25. Paid Mr. Stanley Junior for a cask of Porter had a Month or two ago, £1.1.0., and somebody for the extra work.
> 1792. Jan. 24. Betty Cousins came and was hired £6 per Annum to Martinmas. Betty or Molly Bailey came that day and to have wages £4.10.0, or if she behaves well £5 per annum."[35]

Those were great and prosperous days—new wife, new heir, new lands, new house, new coach and new servants so commonplace that even their names escaped memory. Old Captain Thomas, at Swaith, was also living in some state with a carriage of his own and a manservant in the house.[36]

William's prosperity was based on the surest foundations. It lay all round him in the fields he knew and farmed so well, tended now in the style of the noble Georgian agriculturists. This revolution to the new scientific methods was not made without criticism and scorn from the plodders who farmed as their fathers farmed, and had equally uneconomic returns. There was even trouble with his own conservative farm hands, one of whom he dismissed after recording that he:

> ". . . does not enter into my fresh Modes of Farming or approve of being put out of his own Way."

The times were propitious. William got the benefit of the old as well as the new. The French wars had started, grain and meat were rising in price. At the same time, the industrial revolution was gaining momentum; new machines were voracious for coal. William had the best of both worlds, meat and grain on his fields, eight feet of gleaming coal underneath.

---

[33] Tax Accounts Book, 2nd Quarter, 1791.
[34] 27 Oct. 1791.
[35] She did behave well.
[36] Tax Accounts, 2nd Quarter, 1792.

Coal-getting was destined to be of tremendous importance to the family fortunes. The great need in William's time was to convey it from under his fields to the new industrial centres. As much could be mined as was required. It all could be brought to the pithead; there it was forced to lie until the horses and carts came down the rutted lanes to collect it. It maddened local landowners to think of the enormous prices being paid at the factories not so many miles away. A canal would have solved the problem; barges would move smoothly to the industrial centres, dozens of tons in a single vessel; the watery surface needing no metalling, the toll-gates by-passed. In 1792 the first definite proposals were made. William and other local magnates came to an agreement: the proposed canal was to pass through Wombwell, Brampton, Wath and Swinton, to the Rivers Don and Dearne. The head of water was to come from the Dove, which wound its way through Worsbroughdale and the canal level in passing from Dove to Don was to be maintained by a reservoir formed in the valley just to the south of Houndhill. The cost was originally estimated at £60,000. Cautious William quickly saw how profitable this investment could be: he stopped hoarding his money in safe Government stock and bought shares in the company, £300 for himself, £200 for his mother, and another £200 for his father-in-law.

The Dearne-Dove Canal was not constructed without difficulty. Local landowners objected to the scientific horror going near their lands. A rival company was started and announced that they had found a shorter and better route for a canal. But in 1793 work on the original plan was started[37]: the first £60,000 was soon spent and the subscribers had to subscribe half as much again. William, having made his investment, went back to buying Consols.

Before he had been at Swaith for two years, old Captain Thomas, Ann Rachel's father, died.[38] A funeral consistent with gentility proved expensive.

"1792. Dec. 2.   Paid Shaw & Trudd, Joiners, for Father's Coffin. £4.6.0.
1792. Dec. 19.   Paid Tate, Shuttleworth & Co. their Bill on the Funeral. £6.13.7.
1792. Dec. 29.   Paid Mr. Thos. Hall for furnishing Funeral. £42.13.4.
1792. Dec. 29.   Paid Mr. Jo. Clarke for furnishing Funeral. £17.8.4."

Correspondence still exists on the dismal fripperies of eighteenth century bereavement.

William wrote to Schofield, his jeweller:
"I shall be obliged if you will make and send me nine black Enamel'd Mourning Rings with the following Inscription. 'Thos. Elmhirst Esq. ob. 2. Decr. 1792. AE.63.' I beg you will make them good and handsome, (and let me have them by such conveyance as you find most proper) with your bill in so short a Time as you can: I'll remit you a Draft on Receipt of the Rings and hope you will as mentioned at Ouslethwaite charge me so low as you can afford."[39]

---

[37] *Hist. Wors.*, p. 259.
[38] 2 Dec. 1792.
[39] Dated from Ouslethwaite, 13 Dec. 1792. These rings cost £10 11s. 6d.

The mourning garments for relatives still living in Lincolnshire, Thomas's brother and his nephews, were got in Horncastle; that part of the family went by arrangement to a "Funeral Furnisher & Draper" there, the bill being sent subsequently to William by the furnisher, who wrote:

"I received your favour in due course, and was extremely sorry for the melancholy occasion, accept my most sincere condolence. Agreable to your Order I have forwarded as by the annexed Invoice which I hope you will find correspond with your Wishes."[40]

If William wished the smothering of his wife's relations in black crepe, black flannel, black bombazett, black bombazeen and black fustian, he must have been well satisfied. The entire Lincolnshire contingent was fitted out, in addition, with Best Black Kid Gloves. At least one of these male ghouls, fortunately not an Elmhirst, showed proper respect by garnishing himself with Black Deathheads Coat Buttons. After the funeral old Thomas's will was found to contain no real surprises: his widow at Swaith was left an annuity of £50 and most of the rest of his property passed to his only child, Ann Rachel. Certain small bequests were made in favour of the black tide now receding into Lincolnshire; the arch-mourner studded in Deathsheads carried away with him an annuity of £10. William now had more lands to manage; chief of these was Fulletby, in Lincolnshire, which he controlled in his wife's name; he made a routine of going over there himself, twice a year, to inspect the properties and call on relations; usually he rode over on horseback; the chaise was used when Ann Rachel accompanied him. He lost no time in introducing the newer farming methods, which proved as successful in Lincolnshire as they were in Yorkshire.

By the summer of 1793 Ann Rachel was expecting a second child. William, still dressed in mourning,[41] went for a holiday at Buxton, leaving his wife under the care of their mothers. He settled himself in a hotel there and kept his weekly bills, even after transcribing them into his notebook. He ate every one of his meals in the hotel itself: there are no signs that he ever invited a friend to eat or drink with him, which makes the alcohol consumption noteworthy. A sample for five days is as follows:

"*St. Anns Hotel, Buxton.*
Wm. Elmhurst Esq. from 26th to 31st May '93.

Lodging Room	7.6
Fires	2.6
Servant lodging	2.6
5 Breakfasts	4.2
5 Dinners	7.6
1 Teas	.10
5 Suppers	5.00
Port Wine and Sherry	1.2.6
Malt Liquor	1.6
Servant Eating	12.6
	£3.6.6"

40 Letter from Simpson's of Horncastle.
41 John Earnshaw's Bill. 30 Aug. 1793.

At the end of his stay, in addition to settling the hotel bills, there were other charges: a guinea to be distributed among the hotel servants, ten shillings for the hairdresser for managing the wig and what little went on underneath, five shillings to the ostler, half-a-crown to the "Bath Man", and another half-a-crown to the "Women at Well".

On this, as on all subsequent visits to spas, the whole business was treated with a most deadly seriousness. He fussily made notes of the best books on the subject, noted too the times at which the nauseating draughts of water should be swallowed, starting at half-past seven in the morning, to "operate" at one o'clock. He noted the best side of the streets at which to stay; he recorded the various hotels in the different spas and even the differences in equipment and price of different rooms in these hotels.

By the time master and groom rode back from this depressing holiday, the second baby was almost due. Another son, named Thomas, after the dead captain, his grandfather, was born on 22 June 1793:

> "1793. Sep. 4. Paid Richard Allott for oak chest of drawers in Nursery. £2.5.0.
> 1793. Dec. 18. Paid Saml. Thorpe Esqr. on account of a Pipe of Madeira Wine of wch. I am to have one half. £25.
> 1794. Jan. 17. Paid for Chimneys swept, Kitchin and Servants Room, 4s. Brewhouse and own Office, 2d. Sitting Room, Drawing Room and Children's Room, 6d.
> 1794 Jan. 17. Paid Mr. Iveson for a hat, £1.1.0; for Pomatum, 2s. 6d.
> 1794. Apr. 28. Sent Messrs. Allen to be invested for me in 3 per cent. Consols. £399.11.6.
> 1794. Jun. 5. Sent do. £100.2.0."

Then, among other horse deals, nearly all advantageous, he had to counteract some Sitwell meanness[42]:

> "1794. Sep. 28. Received of Sitwell Sitwell Esq. of Renishaw for a Bay Horse, called Jack, bought as a foal of Mr. Heaton of Epworth, 6th Novr. 1787. £70. Gave his Grooms 10s. 6d. and 2s. 6d. He sent mine 2s. 6d.; I gave mine 2s. 6d. more."

Ann Rachel had a third son at 8.30 in the evening of Wednesday, 10 December 1794. This was Robert, destined almost to ruin the family which now produced him. The child was baptised a few days later,[43] but the christening was postponed perhaps because of his maiden aunt Martha's illness, maiden aunts liking to attend christenings. Poor Martha never recovered and early in the new year her funeral wound its way to Worsbrough Church with the infant Robert in one of the carriages. To save an additional journey he was christened there and then[44]:

> "1795. Mar. 19. Paid Mr. Schofield for 11 Mourning Rings had 5th. Ult. for Miss Martha Elmhirst. £13.15.0."

[42] Osbert Sitwell: *Great Morning*. Macmillans. 1948.
[43] 15 Dec. 1794.
[44] Saturday, 11 Jan. 1795.

Ann Rachel went off by herself, but accompanied by a servant, to Buxton to recuperate.

A new tax arose in those hungry years; this, the Hairpowder Tax, was an attempt to divert flour from the heads of the fashionable to the stomachs of the poor. William kept powdering to the end of his days:

"1795. May 20. Paid Hairpowder Tax for Mrs. E. and Self. £1.2.0.

1795. Jul. 7. Sent Messrs. Allen by Post, to be invested in the Funds. £330.

1795. Oct. 9. Paid Miss F. Hall for her Brother to buy Quack Medicines. £4.14.6."

During these years of settled prosperity, when revolutionary armies, famine and pestilence swept backwards and forwards across Europe, the accounts are packed with little more than farming costs and profits. Everything else was so remote. William joined a local association called the Darton Club[45]; to the annual guinea subscription he was continually having to add the prices of forfeits for non-attendance or for breaking any other of the fatuous schoolboy rules by which grown men like to bind themselves into a herd whether in the Oddfellows, the Freemasons, or the Officers' Mess.[46]

Very much more significant than the Darton Club was his appointment, at the end of 1796, as Deputy Lieutenant of the West Riding of Yorkshire. It was true that the Duke of Norfolk, who signed the commission, seemed to think William lived at a place called Hooselthwaite, but that was a small matter compared with this real tribute to an upright, efficient and extremely successful country gentleman.

In 1797, for the first time, the European war directly affected distant Yorkshire. This time it was not only the imposition of a new tax, fifteen pence yearly for each dog, but there were sudden rumours of a seaborne landing on the Yorkshire coast. The garrison in the country was raised to 15,000 untrained troops led by men with the military experience of William's late father-in-law. The authorities treated the threatened invasion sufficiently seriously to choose zones where all livestock could be evacuated ahead of the famished revolutionaries; other arrangements were made to evacuate children and the infirm.[47] William subscribed twelve guineas towards the upkeep of what was then the Provisional Cavalry. Ann Rachel, rated separately on her Lincolnshire property, paid another six guineas. Other taxes were increasing steadily. The window tax cost William about £20 a year,[48] though the carriage was still assessed at £8 yearly. Then, in addition to all these previous taxes, there was this new one

---

[45] This had no connection with another Darton Club (Wilson's) founded in March 1832, and intended to serve the collieries.

[46] He resigned 10 May 1816. (Annual Pocket Book.)

[47] Hist. Wors., p. 372.

[48] Genn House, 12 windows, 17s. 6d. Swaith, 38, £4 9s. 6d. Ouselthawite, 35, £4 4s. 6d.

on dogs; this reveals an unsuspected horde of the creatures, two lodged with William's mother at Genn House, six with Ann Rachel's mother at Swaith, and no less than ten at Ouslethwaite.

Income tax was added next year, it started modestly enough, costing the Worsbrough Elmhirsts only £28 in all. How little it affected them can be seen:

"1798. Aug. 21. Sent Messrs. Allen in 34 Bank Notes to be invested in 3 per cent. Consols. £480.
1798. Aug. 25. Paid Sheffield Infirmary my Annual Subscription. £2.2.0.
1798. Sep. 11. Paid Mr. James Carr Tax on Armorial bearing, viz.: Mrs. Ann Elmhirst's, £2.2.0; Own, £1.1.0."

This last entry records another new tax levied on all who displayed coats of arms. The guinea was for simple use, as on the fob-seal, and the two guineas for displaying heraldry on the panel of the carriage door.

Meanwhile, after some five years of digging in the valley, the new Dearne and Dove Canal had been completed. A wedge-shaped reservoir covered the rank damp lands in the valley, which had always lain between Elmhirsts quick and Elmhirsts dead. This first year the freight the canal carried was but small; prospects, however, remained excellent for the years ahead when both mines and canal would be geared to higher production.

The eldest child, William, now eight years old, had been sent to the boarding school of a Reverend William Porter, both curate and schoolmaster, who had a popular following among the local gentry whose children he had been boarding and teaching for a great many years. On 4 February 1799 Thomas his brother joined him as a new boy at the same school. A month after the term started the younger boy fell ill; within 48 hours it was decided to take him to Swaith to stay with his grandmother. Young William, too, had just begun to sicken and the two boys left the school together. Four days after they reached Swaith Thomas died[49]; in another twelve days the family grave was disturbed again for young William to join his schoolfellow.[50] What had happened it is not possible to tell. Family tradition says that both boys were lost in Wombwell Wood and then were overfed on their return. It is more probable, if they were so lost, thirsty and hungry, that they drank contaminated water and subsequently died of cholera or typhoid, both of which were then endemic. This horrible incident terribly afflicted the parents. Ann Rachel hoarded a coin merely because it had once belonged to William, and then solemnly bequeathed it to

---

[49] William's Commonplace Book, pp. 11 and 12.
[50] Both were disinterred again later during the earliest Victorian "improvements". The coffins were in the north aisle opposite Robert's vault. (Wm. Elmhirst to Frederick Fisher. 4 Sept. 1838.)

her daughter.[51] William, the father, as had already been noted, actually let a little sentiment creep into his account books and:

> " 'Alas! Alas!' he wrote in the Commonplace book.
> 1799. Jan. 21. Paid Revd. W. Porter for Wm's board, etc. to Xmas 1798 £16.5.6.
> 1799. Feb. 4. Paid for Thomas' Entrance that Day. £2.2.0.
> 1799. Apr. 13. Paid Dr. Chorley for attending my son Wm. etc. £18.18.0.
> 1799. May 11. Paid Mr. Wm. Tootle on Acct. of son Wm's Funeral. £3.17.6.
> 1799. May 11. Paid Mr. Thoas. Hawksworth on Annt. of same, balance of Bill. £14.15.6.
> 1799. Sep. 2. Paid Revd. Mr. Porter for my late dear boys 10 Guineas, Servants 1 Guinea."

Six weeks after young William's funeral, Ann Rachel had another son whom the bereaved parents called William, in the place of his dead brother. So the boy Robert, now about five years old, moved unexpectedly from the third to the first place in the succession. But it was the new-born baby who was destined to lead the family, after Robert's death, back to prosperity by way of cautious respectability and coal.

William's reading matter in these years of early middle age are interesting. He subscribed to three newspapers, *Sheardown's Gazette*, *The General Evening Post* and *The Yorkshire Journal*. His chief interest in these concerned the agricultural market; the most interesting items, the prices of wheat at Doncaster for instance, were copied out for every month from about this time until the end of his life. Prices for other crops and livestock were often added. From the journals, too, he noted hints on foretelling the weather and on treating diseases in animals and humans. His books were few and all entirely improving. Notebook extracts of this period are typical:

> " For a Sore Throat by Dr. C——y [Chorley]. A saline draught with half a Dram of Cordial Confection and a Dram of Tincture of Snake Root.[52]
> "In Rheumatic Weather Take 6 or 8 Drops of Oil of Rosemary every Night before going to Bed, in a Coffee Cup of Cold Water and continuing it during the Winter. The effects will be astonishing.[53]
> "Dr. Blair's Lectures on Rhetoric and Belles Lettres. Printed in London in '83 and indespensably necessary to be studied by every person who wishes to speak and write with Accuracy and Elegance.[54]
> "To form the Character of a Man of Business, Firmness and decision must unit with Good nature and Flexibility.[55]
> "Widow Mitchel says that her Mother's mother was own Cousin to Mrs. Sykes' Mother.[56]
> "Miss E. came from Doncaster, her Eye had been covered to that time; the Accident happened Sat. 31st Augt., therefore the Eye was covered 9 weeks and 4 days.[57]

---

[51] William III crown scratched "W.E. 1797".
[52] Small Pocket Book. 1795.
[53] Small Pocket Book. 1799.
[54] *Ibid.* 1799
[55] *Ibid.* 1799
[56] Small Pocket Book. 1806.
[57] Thick Pocket Book, p. 32. 6 Nov. 1805.

"Preservation of Lambs from Foxes. Equal parts of Black Sulpher, Tar and Train Oil, mix'd with a broad Stick, touch with this Mixture the Gates of the Fields where lambs are kept."[58]

The careful buying of gilt-edged securities still left William with plenty of money. In 1801[59] he agreed to buy, for £5,000, a new house and property in Worsbrough known as Round Green.[60]

Next year, 1802, Robert, perhaps already a problem at eight years old, went to boarding school. Not, this time, to the local parsonage, but to live with a Mr. Haigh in Doncaster.[61] This Haigh was a close relation, probably a son, of the Haigh senior, of Messrs. Caley, Haigh & Pugh, the wine merchants from whom William bought his large quantities of Port and Madeira. Perhaps young Robert got a liking to the smell even from the age of seven.[62]

This choice of a school, particularly because of what came later, is an odd interpretation of William's Views on the Education of Boys in his commonplace book.

"In regard to Boys intended for the Professions, or a Public Life, there can be no Comparison of Advantages: a public Education is undoubtedly best; but a private one is certainly best adapted for Youth in the Walks of Trade or Business. It tends to check Ambition and Extravagance and to give ideas consonant to that moderate Sphere in which by far the greater part of Mankind are doomed to move. Take a Boy from a Public School and place him in Business, he may feel himself degraded. At the University, or in a Public Office, he knows himself to be in his Element."[63]

French invasion was again a possibility. William duly subscribed in the course of a single year to an outing for the local cavalry,[64] to the Army of Reserve,[65] and to the Thorne Volunteers.[66] As the Grand Army blackened the north of France and the barges clustered near Boulogne, such subscriptions became bigger and more frequent. The Yeomanry Cavalry got additional awards "for additional Conveniences"; this fantastic troupe was clothed at this time in scarlet coats, green cuffs and buff waistcoats; on their heads were round hats, crowned with nodding plumes. It would have been interesting to see how these colourful volunteers fared against the French veterans of a dozen campaigns. Then there were the Staincross Volunteer Infantry,[67] the West Riding Internal Defence Committee,[68] the Ecclesfield Parish Volunteers,[69] and something even

---

[58] Thick Pocket Book, p. 38.
[59] Agreement 15 Aug. 1801.
[60] Sold by Robt. Rockley of Rockley to William West for £220 in Feb. 1620. By Eliz. Drake (née West) it was sold to Francis Hall for £640 on 9 Oct. 1690 (Elmhirst MSS.). William bought it from the Halls, who were then kinsmen.
[61] Nov. 1802.
[62] Board and schooling cost about £50 a year. General Accounts.
[63] Commonplace Book, p. 33.
[64] General Account Book. 3 Feb. 1802.
[65] Ibid. 8 Aug. 1803.
[66] Ibid. 24 Nov. 1803.
[67] General Accounts. 18 April 1804.
[68] Ibid. 18 April 1804.
[69] Ibid. 29 Nov. 1804.

had to be paid toward "Captain Bland's Company".[70] Prime Minister Pitt had a great deal of trouble with such volunteers and their much emphasised articles of service. One of the most important terms was that they should never be required to leave the kingdom. Against this paragraph Pitt could not resist writing: "Except in the case of actual invasion."[71]

As Bonaparte poised for his lead, when all Europe held its breath and when England's Fleet was at sea, news came to Barnsley that the invader had landed.[72] Beacons blazed and drums rattled as five hundred Staincross Volunteers poured into the town. After tearful farewells, they started their march at three in the morning to the rendezvous at Hemsworth, where they found a strange lack of enthusiasm. A smouldering field had been mistaken for a beacon and all other local beacons had been fired as a result.[73]

During these anxious days old Elizabeth, William's mother, fell sick at Genn House, where she lived with her lone spaniel, having lost all the others when such livestock were whittled down under the dog tax. After a fortnight's illness she died, having outlived the surgeon-apothecary by more than thirty years.[74]

Ann Rachel had had yet another son, christened Richard,[75] and William's grey mare had given birth to a colt, christened Roscius,[76] destined to become William's favourite.

An answer to William, written by a stud groom, to his questioning as to the previous performance of a mare he had bought, cannot be omitted.

"Yours came safe to His Grace who wood a been Verry Happy to a Given You a more Perticular account than what His Grace is able at Pressant, for His Grace has been most shockingley afflicted with the Gout for some years, and is Very bad at this Pressant time. In 1792 His Grace ordered a Great Number of Horses and Mares for Sale at York, and Pedegreese was given alon with them, amongist which was that of the Dam of your Mare, which I think was got by Paymaster, her Dam by Leviathan, shee never run at York or anywhere else as I remember . . ."

At this time, too, William, perhaps expecting a Frenchman behind every hedge, went to the expense of buying a Spying Glass.[77] Relief from suspense came at last:

"1805. Dec. 16. Paid subscriptions for Battle off Trafalgar. Mrs. E. 3 Guineas. Myself 3 Guineas."

In the period immediately following Trafalgar, he concentrated on sheep raising. Instead of the usual fifty animals, he had collected more than five times

---

[70] General Accounts. 9 June 1804.
[71] Stanhope: *Conversations with Wellington*, p. 113. Oxford. 1938.
[72] 15 Aug. 1805.
[73] *Hist. Wors.*, p. 169.
[74] Mourning rings, gold with black and white enamelling, were given to commemorate the event.
[75] Born 13 Sept. 1803.
[76] Sired by "Tantivy".
[77] General Accounts.

as many in the years between 1806 and 1808. Nor was all the work done by the sheep themselves. His notebooks are plastered with memoranda on sheep breeding and how to differentiate the progeny of one ram from those of another.

Another preoccupation then was the great Enclosure Movement. Not only was he concerned that he got his share of the land, but he was, surprisingly for those times, careful of the rights of others. The technique of enclosure had become systematised. Local landowners, coveting commons and waste lands on which they had rights of pasturage, but which were wasted for intensive agricultural development, banded themselves in an Association. This association of big men with a meek assenting chorus of selected lesser men thereupon petitioned Parliament that that particular stretch of land would be better employed under private ownership. The preamble to the petition to Parliament, which culminated in the enclosure of the Thurgoland commons, was typical of all the others:

> "The Lord of the Manor of Thurgoland and other proprietors there, Walter Spencer Stanhope Esquire, Francis Fawkes Esquire, James Cockshutt Esquire, William Elmhirst Esquire, and several other Persons, Owners and Proprietors of Messuages, Lands and other Hereditaments situate there who are therefore entitled to Right of Common in, over and upon the said Commons believing that it would be of advantage to them if the same were inclosed and divided them in proportion to their respective rights and as such Division cannot be effectually established without the Authority of Parliament now . . ." etc., etc.

William gave all his support to what was then so obviously progress. To think otherwise was to be a Jacobin, a Radical, even an Atheist. It was easy to be sure in those days.

His notebooks filled one after another; the age recorded on the name-plate of a farmhand's coffin was 78, when it should have been 76.[78] A better way to clean top-boots,[79] a good gruel for a horse after hunting,[80] and an excellent emetic for a young hound[81]; and Robert had worn out both his pairs of shoes.

In 1811 the bread William had cast on the waters of the Dearne and Dove Canal returned to him in the form of a first dividend. The dues collected in the year of its opening had only been £458, seven years later they amounted to £2,271, before William died they reached £7,485 in the year.[82] Apart from the excellent dividends, William was even faster enriched by the minerals which were now mined in larger and large quantities from under his lands. In one year the ironstone[83] alone brought him £366.[84]

---

[78] Thick Pocket Book, p. 61.
[79] Ibid., p. 53.
[80] Ibid., p. 63.
[81] Ibid., p. 97.
[82] Company Reports.
[83] Sold under agreement to Richard Swallow (£140 per acre p.a.) dated 10 Oct. 1800.
[84] Small Pocket Book, 1809-10.

Meanwhile, Robert was due to leave Mr. Haigh's school at Doncaster. From this period there survives a geometry book of his, not overthumbed, but fly-leaves well scribbled upon; the self-condemnatory word "Dunce" is the last entry in a mass of scribblings.[85] In 1812, at seventeen, he was articled to Messrs. Wheat to start his law education.[86] At this period James and John Wheat were solicitors in Paradise Square, in Sheffield, and it was probably this place to which he was transferred when he had first been fitted up with smarter clothes and a bright new watch. The boy wasted five years in Paradise Square, the only piece of his work that survives is a badly copied list of Bonaparte's upstart marshals and pasteboard kings that he laboriously transcribed from the newspaper.[87] The holidays alone counted as true living, then there was shooting and riding to hounds.

When Robert was in Sheffield an agricultural gloom settled over England; European and other markets were closed because of Bonaparte's counter-blockade. Grain glutted the markets and in the spring of 1815 a load of wheat fetched only 26 shillings (in 1813 the price had been 44 shillings).

William and Yorkshire generally were very much less interested in Napoleon's career after Trafalgar. Now there was no danger of invasion; the snow of Russia and the running sore of Spain could be relied upon to sap the Corsican's strength. William was more interested in the weight of an American pig that was killed and a good prescription. He did, however, subscribe to a celebration held at Mount Vernon to mark, prematurely, the return of peace.[88] After the escape from Elba and Waterloo, he only recorded:

"Monday, 7th Augt. 1815. Bonaparte went on Board the 'Northumberland,' from the 'Belerophon,' to be taken to St. Helena."

and he noted his arrival off that island on the 16th October.[89]

Meanwhile, the agricultural depression deepened. In the autumn of the year of victory a load of wheat fetched only 25 shillings, in spring, 1816, it had sunk to 20 shillings, less than half what it fetched in a good season. William was a reasonable landlord and for two or three years during the depression he agreed to accept considerably less than usual. Cuts up to 40 per cent. are made in nearly all his rents "in consideration of the bad year for agriculturists".

In the post-war depression, crime was on the increase. Not only had many farm hands become unemployed, but many others, when they had been dis-possessed from the commons by the Enclosure Acts, could no longer maintain

---

[85] Dated 1808-10. Reminiscent of another school book, one of those autographed and left to Worsbrough School by Obadiah Walker, which read: "Harbert Elmhirst his booke but never on it did he looke." Herbert was the son of John, the Fellow of University College. He himself matriculated there on 6 May 1670. *Hist. Wors.*, p. 380, and *Alumni Oxon.*
[86] Articling cost £312. 8 July 1812. Small Pocket Book.
[87] *The General Evening Post.* 14 Jan. 1813.
[88] Small Pocket Book. 18 July 1814.
[89] Thick Pocket Book.

themselves. Added to these hungry unfortunates, there were returning those whom Wellington had called the scum of the earth, those who had enlisted for drink, who had fought in Iberia and France, and who now came home to find themselves untrained and unwanted. William and other landowners had to do something to protect their property against these hungry men and the Royston Association for the Prosecution of Felons was formed. Members of the Association subscribed towards rewards to be paid to informers should their information lead to a conviction; a convicted potato-stealer meant £1 to the informer, a house-burglar meant as much as £20.[90] William, of course, had made notes on his losses. His swollen flocks were raided several times; once he tracked a rogue for a long way, once he found one of the raider's pronged sticks. Young Thomas found the sheep's skins that had been thrown aside and came upon another clue in the form of a handkerchief.[91]

The Worsbrough Enclosure Act was an accomplished fact. Notice of the intending enclosure was published in the local newspaper[92] and the common was soon thereafter carved up among the local potentates. Rights of common pasturage and the ancient playgrounds disappeared under a utility patchwork of hedges and fences. A hundred acres had to be sold to meet the cost of the application to Parliament, and the lords of the two neighbouring manors, Worsbrough and Darley, carried off most of the land between them. William got nearly 20 acres[93] and what was left was shared among the other claimants.

All this time Robert had not been doing too well in Sheffield's Paradise Square. It was decided to send him to a lawyer's office in London. In November 1817 he left for town with £55 in his pocket and at the same time his conscientious brother William was started on his legal training. Robert's new office was that of Mr. George Harrison in Lincoln's Inn,[94] but simultaneously he had some connection with a Mr. Knowles at New Inn[95] and lodged near Euston Square.[96] Here he ran into more trouble of which the details are unknown. Only two documents survive of this period, when Robert was twenty-three in London. One is almost the only piece of legal work he ever did—a draft of a sample prosecution of a poacher which presumably struck him as something which might be useful, as it probably was.[97] The second document is more intriguing in view of his subsequent history. Robert must have offered marriage to an old widow about whom he knew nothing; her answer somehow survived his own natural carelessness and his relatives' acuter sense of scandal:

---

[90] Association Handbill, dated 1 Dec. 1817.
[91] Notes dated Jan. 1819.
[92] *Leeds Intelligencer*. 23 June 1817.
[93] Levelling and fencing these acres cost William £250. Small Pocket Book, 1817-18.
[94] Thick Pocket Book, pp. 133 and 140. No. 8, New Square, Lincoln's Inn.
[95] Address on title page of his Almanac for 1818.
[96] No. 3, Seymour Street, Euston Square. Ann Rachel's Almanac for 1819.
[97] Dated Michaelmas 1818.

"4 America Square,[98]
22d June 1818.

"Sir,

I should deem myself most ungrateful were I to delay for a moment to acknowledge the obliging and flattering sentiments of which you have thought me worthy, and I hope that a further acquaintance would confirm and augment your good opinion, to deserve which be assured is now the warmest wish of my heart, I am nevertheless unwilling to *hasten* any engagement, for it would be prudent to be *certain* that your *judgement hereafter* will *approve*, what has hitherto *captivated* your *fancy*, accept however in the meantime, of my best thanks for the admiration you have expressed, at the next party I have the honor of meeting you I shall hope for the pleasure of an introduction, which I trust we shall find a happy commencement of a long series of years, replete, may we flatter ourselves, with every delight, which the warmth of your attachment may promise, I have had my share of sorrow and woe in this world, I have *twice* been an *afflicted* widow, but this has been far from rendering my heart callous to new impressions, I feel capable of returning your affection with the greatest warmth and steadiness.

"I am left in possession of a sufficiency to supply all our wants with comfort and *indeed with some degree of style*, imagining you have not as yet realized much, I am induced to mention the subject as this might be a source of uneasiness to you,

from your devoted
M. Howard."

This carefully composed letter was addressed to Robert by his last name only: "—. Elmhirst Esq." at Knowles' in New Inn. The only other relic of this whirlwind courtship is a very second-rate anonymous poem, undoubtedly by the same authoress, full of similar sentiments and emphases. One verse will serve to show the nauseating nature of the whole:

"Oh may the auspicious day that *gives you Howard*
Be but the first of a long train of days
Pregnant with blessings, and may Nature's face
So deck'd with smiles but the forerunner be
Of a long life of Joy and Happiness
Of social intercourse and wedded Love!"

A few months after this odd correspondence, Robert went back to Yorkshire. His last year in London (1818) had cost his father considerably more than £400, of which it is safe to assume only a very small amount was spent in legal training.[99] What developed between him and the widow, whether she accepted his offer of marriage, or whether they were even subsequently married, is unknown; at least it is certain that there was no such ceremony in her local church.

William had his prodigal son back in Ouslethwaite with him in May 1819,[100] vainly hoping that farming might prove more to his taste than the law. At the same time, he had started off his second son, William, on his advanced legal

---

[98] America Square lies beside John Street, off the Minories, in the parish of St. Botolph's, Aldgate. In Aug. 1817 James Tunnard, a corn merchant, lived there. (Johnstone's *London Street Directory*, 1817.)
[99] Small Pocket Book, 1818. Robert's account at back.
[100] "After being with Mr. Harrison". Thick Pocket Book, p. 140. On p. 133 is the address: "Geo. Harrison Esq., No. 8, New Sq., Linc. Inn."

training[101] and shortly afterwards his third son, Richard, was apprenticed to a surgeon.[102]

Robert was probably bored after the excitement of London. Two years dragged by. In July 1821 fat George was crowned at Westminster in the place of his mad father. From contemporary almanacs there is a brief glimpse of Robert and William going to a Coronation Ball at Bradford, dancing twenty-three dances and Robert hurrying off next day to a similar celebration at Sheffield.

In this summer old William set off with Ann Rachel and their daughter Ann on the annual tour of his own and his wife's estates in Lincolnshire. They called first at Usselby House to see their cousin Colonel Richard and his family. From there they went on to Skegness where Ann Rachel ventured to take a sea bathe, then they slowly wound their way back to Colonel Richard's. All the way, as was his wont, William was scribbling in his notebooks, wearying his bespectacled eyes. Loose in one of them he carried the year's almanac, a sheet of adhesive plaster useful for small injuries, a small piece of blotting-paper, and a new method of weather forecasting from the *General Evening Post*. Halfway round his tour he wrote to Robert left behind at Ouslethwaite, he told him the family news then moved on to more enthralling topics such as the state of the Lincolnshire crops and the prices of fat cattle:

> "From the weather through the Week I am hoping you are getting busy with Harvest, I shall be glad to hear of your being so. Your Mother is hoping the servants keep steady and that you are not very uncomfortable in our absence."[103]

Three weeks after writing this characteristic letter, when Robert and young William with two friends were returning from the Doncaster Races, their father lay dying at Usselby House. Colonel Richard sent for Robert at four o'clock on a Wednesday morning. The letter was brought by the hand of Geye, the Colonel's servant:

> "You have been informed of your Father's indisposition. I am now grieved to tell you that he is in great danger; in consequence of which your good Mother, my Wife and I think that you should come to Usselby *without loss of time*, indeed the Physician thinks there must be a change either for the better or worse within twelve hours as there has been a material alteration within the last eight hours and I must add, that you may as well be prepared for the most unfavourable intelligence upon your arrival.
>
> "Two Physicians have attended him and everything has been done which we could procure."[104]

Three converged in a hurry upon Usselby House: first came Robert, in at the death, as he no doubt told himself as he rode over. Then there was Birks, the Worsbrough lawyer, who frantically wanted William's approval to a new scheme of an inclined railway running from Worsbrough Bridge through William's

---

[101] First clerkship agreement 15 Dec. 1817. Small Pocket Book 1817.
[102] Letter of Surgeon T. Chorley at Leeds to William, dated 23 Oct. 1820.
[103] Dated from Skegness. 26 Aug. [1821].
[104] [19 Sept. 1821.]

land to the west end of the Dearne and Dove Canal.[105] He had been bombarding
William with letters throughout his Lincolnshire tour and now:

"On my arrival at Usselby I am much concerned to find you are too unwell to attend
to any Business."[106]

Death, the last of the horsemen, reached Usselby at midday on 21 September,
1821.

---

[105] Proposal advertised in *Doncaster Gazette*, 15 Sept. 1810.
[106] Note from Birks, dated 14 Sept. 1821.

GENERATION XIV
ROBERT ELMHIRST OF ROUND GREEN AND ELMHIRST
1794-1835

Robert rode back to Ouslethwaite on the evening of 22nd September 1821 to tell his anxious brother William, who had been trying to find out what had been happening in Lincolnshire, that their father was dead. Preliminary arrangements had to be made for the funeral. Late the next afternoon they went together across the valley to order the preparation of the family vault. Then Robert rode off again, back to Usselby, to bring home his mother and sister. The corpse travelled more slowly; all the sons, Richard having been called from his medical studies and Thomas collected from school, rode out to meet their dead father on Birdwell Common and accompanied him to Worsbrough, where he was laid among his ancestors. The women of the family, as was customary at this time, kept away from the funeral and mourned at home at Ouslethwaite.[1]

It must have been an odd family meeting that autumn. First and foremost, always first and foremost, was the widow, the formidable matriarch, the double Elmhirst, Ann Rachel. She was small and wiry,[2] dominating and imperious; used to having her own way with her inherited property in Lincolnshire; she now expected automatically to control her late husband's estates.

Robert must have felt rather differently about it all. Nominally head of the family, he probably missed no less, in another way, his kind but depressingly efficient father. In spite of their disparity in age, they had had certain interests in common; both appreciated horses, hunting and good wine: the difference lay in the fact that with the father these had been calculated relaxations, while to Robert they were life itself. Law studies made him tired and if he knew next to nothing about estate management, that was because no responsibility had been left to him by his over-zealous parents. A depressing stretch of years lay ahead, marooned in that big house at Ouslethwaite with little to do except avoid his mother's watchful eye. Shooting and riding, even rent-collecting, offered some consolation; he could then pretend he was independent and really Squire; in this way, too, he could meet others of his own jolly sort.

By his father's will, Robert inherited all the Yorkshire properties and from these estates he was to allow his mother £100 a year. She naturally retained the Lincolnshire lands that she had brought with her on her marriage. There were a great many debts to be settled; Robert was shown a rather disturbing list, which he signed, totalling nearly £5,000; a great part of this was not as

---

[1] William E's. Almanack for 1821. Funeral was on 27 Sept. 1821. (Wors. Par. Reg.)
[2] Diaries record her minute weight.

bad as it seemed. His father had borrowed £1,619 from his wife, another £420 from Robert's Aunt Elizabeth (Taylor), and £58 from Colonel Richard Elmhirst, in whose house he had died. However, there were Robert's brothers' and sisters' school bills still unpaid (£100), various servants (£50), and the Commissioners concerned in the enclosures of Thorne and Bradfield (£280). Even the grocer wanted nearly £50. To meet all these commitments it was decided to sell six hundred acres of the land that William had inherited from Mordecai Cutts in 1787. The property was split into twenty-seven lots and was to be auctioned at the White Hart at Thorne about the first anniversary of the funeral.[3] This sale was never completed. Some lots remained, presumably because the reserve prices were not reached; four years later Robert was still trying to dispose of some of the lots,[4] others remain in the family to this day. Nor were William's debts ever to be cleared in Robert's lifetime: he was soon to be fully occupied in trying to satisfy his own creditors.

For a year or two Robert tried to be as good a landlord as his father had been. He even conscientiously subscribed to "A Treatise on the Culture and Management of Fruit Trees,"[5] and he very quickly got a bruised and swollen face from a poacher he had caught on his lands.[6] For a little while, too, he gave his legal advice to his mother and his Aunt Elizabeth; after he, or they, tired of this, the only legal textbook he bought was a pamphlet on the Game Laws.[7]

In July 1824 he broke his leg,[8] which, according to the surgical practice of the time, kept him abed until well into the hunting season: he amused himself by designing a special shockproof cover to be worn when riding to hounds.[9] Brother William had spent that long summer and autumn arranging to get married. His wife was Anna Walker, the granddaughter of a one-time apprentice of Surgeon-apothecary Elmhirst; in spite of this it was a prosperous marriage. Her parents lived, or rather resided, at Swinnow Park near Wetherby.[10] Soon after their marriage the young couple moved out of Yorkshire to their first home in Lincolnshire.

This wedding meant that Robert was more than ever isolated. His next brother, Richard, was seven years younger, a great gap at that age; anyhow he was still away, studying medicine. Robert's mother never now asked him his opinion on anything, at least no single document survives which he composed or wrote for her; every one of them, and they are many, are in her own hand or in young William's.

---

[3] 4 p.m. Wednesday, 25 Sept. 1822. (Printed Sale Catalogue.)
[4] Robert offered Lot 11 for £1,200 on 14 Jan. 1826.
[5] By Chas. Harrison. F.H.S. Subscription copy. London. Printed for the Author, 1823.
[6] Benj. Winder sentenced to 3 months, 29 Sept. 1821. (William's Almanack.)
[7] Letter to Knowles. 22 March 1824.
[8] 5 July 1824. (William's Almanack.)
[9] Draft letter to Messrs. Grayhurst & Harvey, 4 Sept. 1824.
[10] Married 9 March 1825.

At the burial of his maternal grandmother, the widow at Swaith, one catches a brief glimpse of another family funeral gathering and Robert's last public appearance before his revolt. Even in the list of mourners he was subordinate: it was "Mrs. Elmhirst and Mr. Elmhirst," and never the other way round. Robert, as the eldest grandson, was arrayed in a black silk scarf, black hatband and gloves. The full-blooded rococo blackness of the earlier family funerals had given way to something deader and duller; there was a strict social filter through which only black gloves fell to the lot of servants, the six bearers were treated to black hatbands as well as gloves while only the clergy achieved the distinction of getting the full outfit without the price of blood relationship. Robert ordered the mourning rings and sent his jewellers some of the old lady's hair to be made into a mourning brooch.[11]

He managed about this time to settle his London debts, some of which were probably outstanding since those wild days in town. He sent a lump sum to Knowles, the lawyer who was his friend and tutor, and then wrote to all the tradesmen who had been dunning him, telling them to apply to the offices in New Inn.[12] Thus, temporarily relieved he incurred, in the best Corinthian style, a new series of bills by ordering six pairs of white hunting breeches, for which he had given the most meticulous details as to the siting of the buttons.[13] Then two more gigs had been bought and one among many guns[14]:

> "Mr. Tate, Gunsmith,—You have at last forwarded my Gun to this place when I had given up all expectations of seeing it. If you can in any moderate time send me the charge of *shot* I shall have a day's Rook shooting, it is of no use having the charge of *powder* without knowing the quantity of shot."[15]

And a patent chopping machine for the farm at Round Green, one of the rare occasions when he turned his disastrous attention to agriculture, which led to another letter in a similar tone:

> "Mr. Kynman, if you are not here before Saturday I shall send all your Men home, they in my absence had two holes cut in the Walls and left without any Props, it is quite shameful and appears as tho' you wished and was determined to have the building come down, rest assured I shall be as good as my Word and perhaps better."[16]

Robert was soon once more in debt; he wrote again to his friend Knowles who had just settled the last of his London accounts:

> "Now my good Sir pray give one thought to the situation you are placing me in, I never once supposed you could be in the situation your letter would give me reason to believe. I must say I feel it of essential consequence raising the wind to fulfil my engagements."[17]

---

11 Draft letter to Messrs. Grayhurst, 28 March 1826, *et seq.*
12 Series of letters dated 14 Jan. 1826.
13 Draft letter to Richard Clark, Newark. 18 Jan. 1826.
14 Draft letter to Messrs. Slade, London. 28 March 1826.
15 Letter dated 2 May 1826.
16 Draft letter dated 7 March 1825.
17 Draft letter dated 13 March 1826.

To offset new expenses Robert decided to get rid of the clerk whom he had employed to manage the legal side of his affairs and who consequently was doing little else than managing ordinary correspondence. From now onwards, as Robert did his own letter writing, drafts are scarce, accounts and records practically non-existent: those who knew him well realised that his letter writing was a seasonal occupation. "As I found last winter," wrote his Cousin Will, "it was impossible to get an answer from you in the height of the hunting: I have deferred writing till it was rather on the decline."[18] His brother Richard did not even expect an answer in the spring and knowing that any alternative to writing would be taken, "as the hunting season must ere this have terminated with you, you would probably prefer mounting your horse and favouring me with your company."[19] It was with his kinsman, Colonel Richard Elmhirst in Lincolnshire, that he most regularly corresponded; moreover, he kept a selection of these letters that came from time to time from the older man with whom he had nearly everything in common and on whom he seemed to have modelled himself in his earlier years.

"My dear Robert,
This morning soon after six Richard left Usselby and reached Louth in good time for the Mail. We were much obliged to him for his Company which we wish we could longer have enjoyed. You are a Father to him, and I've no Doubt of his being fully sensible of your affectionate kindness; he is a very steady nice young man and will do well in the World.
Richard enjoyed Foxhunting on Monday; we met at Swallow crossroads, found in a few minutes in one of those two gorse covers, the Fox ran up wind and the scent being good, there was a run for about 2¼ miles to another cover whence he had as narrow an escape as ever a Fox had.
On Wednesday we had a capital course between Clarissa and Dr. Syntax, the former was the fastest tho' the Dog ran well, the blue Bitch Violet also ran a good course against Brunette but from her accident she cannot run.
The Bay Mare I think has lost her Vein from bleeding and she is grown too tall.
Best thanks for the Pointer but as she is not ready to break I shall be thankful for your keeping her a few months."[20]

It was probably at the end of 1825 or early in 1826 that Robert changed the course of his own and others' lives. Legend asserts that after a hard day's riding he brought back a friend with him to Ouslethwaite, intending to entertain him as a friend should be entertained by a gentleman of his acquaintance. His mother had different ideas and had nothing more exciting than boiled mutton and caper sauce set before them. This was food that Robert loathed at any time, but now he was being humiliated before his friend and in what was technically his own house. He flung himself out of the Hall and went down to the smaller house at Round Green where at least he could be undisputed master and where the staff would look to him for orders and not wait for the word of

[18] William Elmhirst of Roughton to Robert E., 4 March [1834].
[19] Dr. Richd. Elmhirst to Robert E., 27 April 1834.
[20] Col. Richard E. to Robert, 3 Feb. 1825.

the matriarch. An apocryphal version of the story adds that, to be sure that meals should be more to his taste in the future, he took with him one of the servants called Sally Baxter, from Ouslethwaite, who was young and adaptable; she would have been twenty-one then and could do other things beside cook.

As far as contemporary evidence is concerned, it all, from the addresses, suggests that from this time, February 1826 at the latest, he was living at Round Green that was to house him for the rest of his life. Whether the breach with his mother was complete and final, it is more difficult to say; no correspondence, if there ever was any, has survived between Robert and his mother. Colonel Richard alone seems to have kept his friendship unimpaired, even though later in his life he never hesitated to write exactly what he thought. It is even more difficult to discover the real truth concerning Sally Baxter: certainly she was living with Robert in 1831, when she was twenty-five and he thirty-seven; but whether she was indeed the ex-cook of Ouslethwaite or a housekeeper, later employed at Round Green, or somebody he met in Sheffield or Doncaster, it does not seem possible to say. The respectable were very thorough in eliminating records that contained her name.[21]

In his 1826 almanac Robert was calculating the length of stair-carpeting and the floor measurements of his own and other rooms, by the next year Round Green was being largely rebuilt, with emphasis on stables, carriage houses and kennels.

Meanwhile, he was spending money more freely in other directions, in spite of "Dear Knowles, I am as poor as a Man well can be, you must really do something for me, pray recollect your promises."[22] Typical were the new saddle he ordered for himself in June 1827, together with a more significant woman's side-saddle.[23] Rugs and Turkey carpets were ordered for Round Green, not, of course, to be paid for till the tradesman was on his knees. Then the whole of the house was repainted from top to bottom; even the shooting brake was redecorated white on the inside and a tasteful green on the exterior.[24] A wine merchant at Hull sold Robert twelve dozen bottles of port with no stronger persuasion than by writing that it was "of the same quality as what I forwarded a short time ago to Colonel Elmhirst." Robert and the old Colonel were never closer friends than at this period.

"A Capital Day with Lord Yarborough[25] yesterday; this morning I feel rather stiff or would have the pleasure of seeing you at Horncastle."

---

[21] Sally was not related to the Baxter family at Penistone. A grand-daughter of hers, who was still alive in 1941, said that Sally's brother was a brewer at Thornton-le-Moor, Northallerton, but contemporary Directories offer no confirmation. (Personal commns.) She went to Sheffield after Robert's death. It is of course possible that she was a young widow. In the 1851 Census, as Mrs. Sarah Jennings, of Tickhill, she stated she was born at Richmond, in Yorkshire.

[22] Robert to Knowles, 5 June 1827.

[23] 2 June 1827.

[24] Decoration bill of £108 finally settled, 31 Aug. 1829.

[25] Master of the Burton Hunt in Lincolnshire. (*Sporting Magazine*, July 1830.)

The senior Yahoo in Lincolnshire and he both spoke the same language; neither had much interest in anything but hunting, coursing and shooting. Legend makes Robert a fearless rider (this year he fractured his collarbone),[26] he broke his horses himself, a groom going ahead towing the new animal with Robert, surely red with fury and port,[27] on its unwilling back. A portrait of his favourite hunter remains.[28] The greatly enlarged stables at Round Green, which were big enough on one occasion to shelter the Badsworth Hunt, were partly mechanised by an ingenious device of ropes and pulleys by which Robert, waking early on a hunting morning, by pulling a cord in his bedroom could be sure that a measured quantity of breakfast would tumble before each horse in good time for an early start.[29] More interesting psychologically and more substantial are the intensely moral iron bars which separate the servants' quarters, men from women.

Together with hunting and coursing there was, of course, shooting. Fishing, the third of the bucolic trinity, was too slow and solitary.

> "Yesterday I got out shooting and bagged 9½ brace of Partridges and a Hare: *also shot a Cat.*"[30]

The italics are of the Colonel's own choosing. Later:

> "I have had a Violent Rheumatic Attack from having dress'd for Dinner when extremely hot by shooting; am better tho' still much troubled in one Hip and Leg. Bessy Bedlam won the Cup at Lincoln on Friday absolutely in a common Gallop against Robin Hood. She had not recovered from the effects of the Physic at Doncaster, she is the most beautiful Galloper I ever saw, and uncommonly fast.
>
> From Doncaster Races we got home very well after the St. Leger.
>
> The Duke of St. Albans and Whiting York are to be the stewards next year. Col. King asked me to be one with the Duke, but as you would suppose, I declined. I have shot better this season than of some years, but am now nearly unable to walk. I like the appearance of Cupid he improves by getting finer, Charles managed to let a gate *clap* upon the end of his tail which has hurt his present appearance, he has now a dose of Physic in him; fix a time to come here to shoot."[31]

Meanwhile, there had been two events in the family. In January 1827 brother William's wife had given birth to their first-born, another William, and Robert had gone to be godfather at the christening. A little later sprightly and affectionate Aunt Elizabeth Taylor died[32] and was buried, again the bills were surprisingly kept which is particularly fortunate since on this occasion the bills are headed with a notable engraving representing a high-class funeral on its way to an isolated church. Mourning cloaks were hired, presumably

---

[26] 3 March 1829. (William Elmhirst's Almanac.)
[27] This is guesswork. But he drank port in enormous quantities and more than 850 unopened bottles were counted at Round Green after Robert's death. (William's Inventory, 3-14 Dec. 1835.)
[28] Thought to be called "Carpet Weaver", but more likely to have been sired by that stallion which Col. Richard owned many years before.
[29] Nothing now remains of this contrivance but an idle pulley rusting on a gate-post.
[30] Col. Richard to Robert. Undated, but from Usselby, *i.e.*, before 1829.
[31] Col. Richard to Robert. 28 Sept. 1828.
[32] Aunt Elizabeth's cousin, to Robert. 22 June 1828.

so that the tenants could eclipse their working clothes, at a florin apiece; yards of black crepe had to be bought for the mutes and fourteen black silk hatbands, each two yards long, trailed behind fourteen mourners of significance. In spite of all the trouble he took in burying the old aunt with dignity, "correct and proper" as he put it, and in spite of his marshalling the ten mutes, Robert did not find his finances much improved. He had the coal valued in its Silkstone bed and for a long time thought of selling it all for about £12,000,[33] then he hesitated, thinking it might be worth more even though so deeply placed, and held back at the last moment. For a short while longer he was able to forget his troubles in the usual way. Wrote the Colonel:

> "Do let us see you next week, or the *moment* the weather shall change. Could you send a brace of Gryehounds to your Out-quarters? Yesterday I saw a very fine young Pig, what is call'd a Gilt likely to become a beautiful Sow. The red Bitch Clara I think of keeping at Usselby, she is very promising to *Fly*."[34]

Two months later:

> "Pray who is the Gentleman possessing the Grey Horse, of which you was speaking, a remarkably good Hunter, I think you said he was an Apothecary and wished to part from his Horse. I mentioned the Horse to Sir Robt. Sheffield who said he should like to have him from my description. Would you be so good as see the Horse; observe his Legs and Feet and ask the price.
>
> "My Bitch by Dan out of Daphne is likely to be *very superior*; at present the Dog is like old Dan very *full of Point*.
>
> "I don't like this Catholic business, yet if could believe that they would go no farther I should like to grant so far as the present Bill, but I have not the least Faith in them. If the present *Indulgences* should be granted and they not afterwards be satisfied, we must go *Slap Dash* at them at once and settle the matter."[35]

Colonel Richard had attained sporting fame by breeding a fine trio of grey-hounds, all in the same litter from his old lame bitch called "Brunette"; they were called "Balloon," "Brunette" and "Blue Ruin," and were depicted in an elegant engraving in the *Sporting Magazine* of January 1830: "They are allowed to have greater speed than any three greyhounds in the kingdom of the same litter, and have also shewn most superior bottom." There was a dreadful occasion when one of these wonderful creatures was tricked out of a prize in the most blackguard manner. The Colonel's bitch, "Brunette":

> "gave the Red one a comfortable straightforward *go by*, the Whole Field saw it."

The unhappy hare was killed at the water's edge, the assistant judge "a scamp quite drunk" admitted to seeing nothing while his senior

> "the Judge was stuck fast in one of the Drains and only saw the first turn. There really was not one Person in the Field, above 150, who did not think that Brunette ought to have had the Course.[36]
>
> "Have you any objection for Balloon to appear in the Sporting Magazine as a Stallion

---

[33] Mr. Charlesworth to Robert E. 3 Aug. 1829.
[34] Col. Richd. E. to Robert. 14 Jan. [1829].
[35] Roman Catholic Emancipation. The Colonel was broadminded compared with the King: "I count any man my personal enemy who proposes any such measure."
[36] This must have been the second heat for the St. Leger Stakes of the Louth Coursing Meeting in Nov. 1829. (*Sporting Magazine*, Jan. 1830, p. 217.)

at five sovereigns per Bitch? I thought advertizing him would be the best Plan and to be at Round Green. You, of course, must take the 5 Sovs. for each."[37]

Colonel Richard's eldest son, Will, was more of Robert's own age: a letter from him throws an oblique light on the latter's way of life:

"Nothing would give me greater pleasure than to be at Wheats Hotel to meet you and Sir Tatton,[38] but I really cannot afford it, it would cost a great deal of money to be there with 3 horses for a week, you know I am not now as formerly and besides there are so many naughty temptations."[39]

In the season 1830-1831, Robert obtained shooting rights over the Midhope Moors from Lord Macdonald, who was Lord of the Manor of Midhope; the consequences were to be troublesome to almost everybody concerned. Robert determined to preserve the game; he hired wardens and gamekeepers and set up a private police force of twenty of his own men to keep out poachers and trespassers (which meant everybody except himself and his friends). In addition to this private force he got himself allotted an expensive posse of constables from Sheffield. To offset all these costs he had already formed the Midhope Game Association: fifteen of his friends, including his brothers William and Richard, subscribed £10 a year and in return for this they received a printed Association card signed and sealed by Robert, and a list of the regulations that he had compiled. If any of the members thought it meant anything more than that they would now have to pay instead of being invited for shoots they must have been disillusioned by Rule One : "That Mr. ELMHIRST be Treasurer and have the entire Management."[40] In May 1832, by which time Robert had hoped to have the Moors better organised, all his plans were nearly upset by the interference of Macdonald's steward, who had already infuriated Robert exactly a year before by trying to turn off one of Robert's employees. This time the Steward took advantage of old Lord Macdonald's death and had had the temerity to advertise that the Moors were now to let. Robert sent a fiery letter to Macdonald's heir and continued to use Midhope as formerly. By now, however, the news that the Moors were unoccupied had spread to the local inhabitants who again began to use the place (which until recently had been a free common and unenclosed), as though they had a right to it, walking over it, coursing their wretched dogs which played havoc with the game, even impudently shooting. Robert wrote to a relation of the steward to see if he could settle things between them. He told him of all the difficulties and the rabble all over the place:

"I had the pleasure of walking near 100 yards with a double-barrelled Gun cocked and presented at my body and the Man swearing he wd. blow my Guts out, besides being in a Mob for some time."

---

[37] This advertisement never appeared because the Colonel almost immediately sold "Balloon" to Sir J. Johnstone "at a great price" (Sporting Magazine, Jan. 1830). But "Blue Ruin's" service, at the same price, were available at Roughton Hall, near Horncastle, and were advertised from Jan. 1830 to Feb. 1831.

[38] Sir Tatton Sykes was Sheriff of York about this time and, more importantly, he was Master of his own Hunt. (Sporting Magazine, July 1830.)

[39] William Elmhirst to Robert E. Undated but paper is watermarked 1827. This William married in 1829 and his reformation presumably dated from about that period.

[40] Regulations. Printed by G. Harrison, in Barnsley.

But Robert had, he said, been fighting back and got several convicted at Sheffield for poaching, "in fact there was not one that got clear". He then asked that the recipient of the letter should talk to the steward "to give a lift to an explanation" and closing with an ungracious reference to a past kindness:

"You would confer an obligation upon me which I trust you will not feel too great a trouble when I remind you that I introduced you to Mr. Hartingdon at the Time you was wishing to procure an Appointment at Howden. I shall be at Home till the 18th when I am going to stay a few days at Lord Hawke's, Winersley or Pontefract, the Hounds will then be hunting the Selby country if you could write to either place I should be obliged to you."[41]

A short while later Robert was writing direct to the steward:

"You will allow me to express the astonishment I felt a short Time ago on being told by a Sheffield shooter that you last year when on the Midhope moors gave him permission then and there to hunt his Dogs, had I known the fact on the 12 Aug. I must confess I shd. have looked for the numbers that swarmed on the moors and had not been surprised at my and the keeper's Lives being in danger."[42]

The steward coldly answered that Robert's letter, unless misdated (as it was) had taken thirty-three days to reach him and he never gave anyone permission.[43] As the shooting season approached relations fortunately became more cordial; this time Robert was determined that nothing should go wrong. He arranged for the force of constables to be present a week before the Twelfth: printed notices were erected around the moor's boundaries and all the game-keepers were warned to keep alert. But in spite of the preparations there were plenty of incidents on the great day. Hundreds of people came out on the moors to do exactly what they liked, never was a shoot more distracted with top-hatted policemen bobbing up and down, greyhounds streaking backwards and forwards, guns popping here and there, grouse flying, dizzy and deafened, in all directions around Robert and his friends who were in transports of fury.

A spate of summonses poured out. An anonymous letter that came later to Round Green was of some assistance[44]:

"Having been informed that you was grightley [by greatly out of frightfully?] Insulted upon the Moors on the 12th of August by a party this is to inform you that John Merrell, Forkmaker, Harvest Lane, Sheffield, was one of the foremost among them I had it from his own mouth on Tuesday the 13th. Excuse signing the full name, but if the above is found correct I will then come forward as he greightley insulted me in taking up for Mr. Elmhirst."

Robert kept a list of the names of some thirty people due to be summoned; some were merely trespassing, some had no guns, another had a gun in his pocket,

[41] Robert to George Earnshaw. 9 March 1833.
[42] Robert to William Earnshaw. 3 July (Aug.) 1833.
[43] William Earnshaw to Robert. 10 Aug. 1833.
[44] "John" to Robert. 18 Aug. 1833.

another even had the impudence to point his firearm at the gamekeepers. Then there were two men, both anonymous, though they were traced later, one of whom "had a green jacket on, he was aged," who had the weak excuse that he was looking for a liver-coloured bitch, and a man "said to be a clerk, who had large black Whiskers". Perhaps most irritating of all to Robert were the publicans: no less than three were caught selling beer to the rabble which poured on to the moors. Against this list of marked men Robert scribbled the penalties subsequently inflicted by the magistrates. Noteworthy were his legal tactics: he invoked the recent Enclosure Act to preserve his new grouse moor. Legally he was entirely successful, at least against shooters and shepherds, who were ultimately expelled from what had been the commons, and Robert's precedent was widely followed.[45] Even then his troubles were not over, because of the bilberry pickers from Sheffield. On one famous occasion he ordered his keepers to grab the fattest picker, throw her to the ground and drag her by the legs across the bilberry bushes in an attempt to teach her who was who and what was what; contemporary lack of undergarments must have made the journey both painful and embarrassing but the effect on the other pickers was probably only transient.[46]

For the fourth recorded time during his short spell as head of the family, Robert was again frantic for money. He wrote to the Colonel:

"I can assure you it is with no little concern I have to address you on the subject of Money, feeling it can't be an agreeable one to you and I have so very often, on having the pleasure of seeing you, named the subject much against my inclination."

He went on to ask for the repayment of a loan of about £1,500, saying that the bank was now badgering him because of an overdraft, and suggested that the Colonel might like to make out bills payable in two, three and four months' time.[47] This appeal was answered in a manner no less stilted, the Colonel said he never could make out such drafts because, the assumption is, he might not be able to meet them when they fell due:

"I have always (I trust) held a high and respectable situation in the Country, it is my most anxious desire to continue in that sphere where I have hitherto moved, and am confident that you would be one of the last Men in the World to countenance anything which might have an unpleasant tendency towards me."

After this dignified posturing, he went on to suggest that he might be able to mortgage something if Robert was not willing to do so. Anyhow, Robert should come over for conversations: he thawed to his natural kindly self— Christmas and conversations should go together:

"I can shew you some capital shooting. I have been engaged two days upon a highway Robbery by 3 Men near Fillingham who stop'd a Man on the Highway before 5 o'clock

---

[45] Robert's attempts to preserve the Moors, "no better for their size in the Kingdom," which culminated in the brawlings of 12 Aug. 1833, are mentioned in John Dransfield's *History of Penistone*, 1906 (p. 294). Here the trespassers and poachers are held to be the aggressors, mauling three of Robert's employees so severely that one, John Marsden, subsequently died of his injuries.
[46] Evidence of Charles E., who probably heard it from his Uncle James (1830-1919).
[47] Draft letter. Robert to Colonel Richard. 6 Dec. 1831.

in the afternoon, pulled him off his Horse and Rob'd him, they were yesterday committed for trial and no doubt will be convicted; two confess'd. I had a good days
shooting on friday, shot three brace of Cock Pheasants, 3 Hares and a couple of Wood-
cocks and could have shot more.''[48]

Crime and shooting were also combined in a possession of Robert's which
is still in existence. He had a small leather drinking cup which was to be found
in the gun-box on every Twelfth: there it remained, revealed at each anniversary
for more than a century. This utensil was made of the skin of Mary Bateman,
the notorious murderess hanged at York.[49]

On top of his financial troubles and the bickerings over the Midhope shooting,
things were getting rather complex at Round Green itself. On 8 June 1832
Sally Baxter had given birth to Robert's son, Henry. If Sally did not go away
to have the child, she certainly went away soon afterwards, because there is
extant a most righteous letter from the Colonel to Robert's respectable brother
William:

"My dear William, I think you judged right, after what you had heard of the *Lady's
Departure*, in not sending my letter; I shall now write a congratulatory Letter, with a
few remarks to prevent a reinstatement of the infamous Woman in her *old Apartments*.''[50]

A great many inferences can be drawn from this: that Sally's presence, or
more probably her obvious pregnancy, had so offended the family that the Colonel,
who was also the eldest Elmhirst, had been intending to give Robert a few hints
on respectable appearances. Again, Sally, and this is known to be the truth,
was anything but a nonentity, no poor deluded girl, but an infamous Woman.

The hopes of the relatives were dashed. Sally soon reappeared at Round
Green, infamous and fecund as before. The family was shaken to its foundations,
Ouslethwaite the epicentre; the garrulous flow of letters from the Colonel
seems suddenly to have dried up. Will wrote a dreary letter about sheep to
"Dear Robert," the man who had always before been his cousin Bob; he did,
however, send both his and his wife's best love.[51] Robert himself seems to
have broken contact with this his least critical relative. Kind Will tried
again:

"Dear Robert,—You are I find *playing the old game* and are determined not to direct
a letter to this place. I cannot help contrasting the present time with the past, and calling

---

[48] Col. Richard to Robert. . 21 Dec. 1831.
[49] Most of her criminal life, as confidence trickster, charm-seller and abortionist, was spent in Leeds. She
owned a hen which laid an egg inscribed with the words "Crist is coming" (*sic*). Encouraged by the eggs
reception, she stuffed other prophetic eggs into the creature for subsequent laying. In May 1807 she poisoned
William Perigo and his wife Rebecca, corrosive sublimate in their honey, when a trick was due to be exposed
by them. Mr. P. survived under the care of Surgeon Thomas Chorley, who was an Elmhirst acquaintance.
Mary was hanged 17 March 1809, her body sent for dissection to Leeds General Infirmary, which earned £30
by charging the curious 3d. to view the body. (*Life of Mary Bateman, the Yorkshire Witch*. 2nd Edtn., Leeds.
[1809].)
[50] Colonel Richard to William Elmhirst. 12 Sept. 1832.
[51] 5 Sept. 1832.

to mind the times when there was scarcely a fortnight without either writing or receiving a letter from each other, do turn over a new leaf."[52]

Unhappy Robert was too far gone and perhaps too proud to want to rejoin his family. He decided to raise money on his home at Round Green, in this way none of them need learn about it. In September 1832 he mortgaged it to Lord Howard of Effingham for £3,000, with the proviso that he should continue to live there and that he could redeem it at any time for the same sum with an additional 5 per cent. per annum. Everywhere there was more trouble, even his hunt, the Badsworth, was hundreds of pounds in debt; he helped organise a fund to buy the hounds by subscribing 25 guineas. Then the Midhope Shooting Association disintegrated; censorious friends, his relatives, and doubtless some that were only tired of his dogmatic muddling and the entire absence of any form of balance sheet, nearly all resigned.

Soon Sally was again pregnant and Sophia, a daughter, was born on 12 February 1834, at Round Green. Robert gave up. His name hereafter appeared in William's careful accounts only once when, early in 1835, he paid for Robert a subscription for the Hunt Dinner. His other brother, Dr. Richard, sent him a reminder, not by any means the first, that a remittance would be more than useful; in this letter the roof is lifted off Round Green. He had supposed, the Doctor wrote, that he could have relied on his eldest brother's sense and fraternal feelings, but:

"I fear I have been much mistaken in this supposition and so beg to state what I heard. It is reported that your servants are in the habit of taking spirits at night; and that wine is frequently produced and that healths and toasts are drunk during your temporary absence from home, I will not hurt your filial feelings by informing you of one of the latter which was drunk with great glee.

"Of the number of strangers that are admitted upon your premises during your absence, I conclude you are made acquainted, and of the quantity of provisions that they consume. If you have sufficient resources to defray these unneccessary expenses, I must beg to tell you that I consider it excessively cruel, unkind and also unbrotherly not to grant me an occasional remittance."[53]

One wonders whether Sally presided at these orgies, gleefully drinking perdition to the old hag at Ouslethwaite; or perhaps, some solitary Bacchante, she retired with a bottle to her room, leaving the uproar unchecked, knowing her status and her authority were equally uncertain.

In 1834 Robert's life was enlivened by acting as a second for a duel. It started, as did so many of these ridiculous quarrels, at a polling booth.[54] Robert's friend, Fisher,[55] was going in to vote when an offensive man called John Pearson

[52] Undated. Watermark 1831
[53] Dr. Richard Elmhirst to Robert Elmhirst. 27 April 1834.
[54] This was the first W.R. Election since the Reform Bill of 1832. Robert voted for John Wortley. (Election Poll Books.)
[55] Very probably this F. Fisher was Robert's lawyer friend, who helped him make his will.

said: "I object to Mr. Fisher's vote on the ground of his being a paid agent." Fisher answered that "Billy Pickering might have made such an objection." (Billy Pickering being presumably someone who had had unpleasant dealings with John Pearson.) This apparently mild reply infuriated Pearson, who wrote to demand an instant apology. Fisher, always meek, an improbable friend for Robert, answered mildly that he was not intending to apologise and that Mr. Robert Elmhirst, who was aware of all the circumstances, would act for him and could be seen at Doncaster on Saturday morning. Pearson's second went to Doncaster to meet Robert on that morning, but never found him: he wrote to Fisher:

> "After having remained at the appointed place [the Turf Tavern in Doncaster] from seven o'clock this morning till four P.M. without receiving a visit from your friend, I must confess that I felt not less surprised than disappointed in being frustrated in the attempt to bring this affair to a final issue."

Fisher replied that Robert would be over later in the evening. Actually, Robert arrived at the Turf Tavern at ten minutes past six, heard that Pearson's second had just left to catch the Sheffield coach, hurried to the Ram Inn, whence the coach started, looked inside and on top of the vehicle, and failed to find the other second. They met at last in Sheffield to make arrangements for the duel. It was fixed for the very next morning at 3.30 a.m. on the new Coach Road near Wentworth House. Pearson and Fisher were to fire at twelve paces, Robert to say "Ready" and "Fire". The seconds then set their watches and went off to tell the principals.

Between this moment and dawn the next morning someone must have realised that what seemed very gallant and dashing in the Turf Tavern was not likely to be so amusing in the cold half-light of an impending dawn. Somebody told the police. Which of the four it was will never be known; the one thing about which one can be absolutely sure, was that it was not Robert; there is nothing he would have enjoyed more than a duel and anyhow, though this would not influence him, he was not the target at which anyone was shooting. It may have been the inoffensive Fisher, but by far the most probable informer is Pearson. It was he that had been the cause of the trouble; he was the blusterer and he the challenger. Pearson's second sent off an express letter to Robert:

> "When we were about to leave Doncaster we were stopped by the civil officers, and summoned to appear before the Mayor. It is with the deepest regret that I inform you Mr. John Pearson was bound over to keep the peace. I therefore feel called upon to send you an express to acquaint you with this information, by way of preventing any further trouble to you and Mr. Fisher."

This got Robert out of bed. He dipped his pen in gall:

> "Sir,—During the night your Express called me up. I doubt not you and Mr. John P. found the 'civil officers' 'very civil.'"

Later, however, he seemed to have reconsidered the draft, crossed it out and wrote a more diplomatic reply, still keeping the civil officers in inverted commas. He, at least, seemed to have no doubt that Pearson himself had called the police. The mayor had bound over John Pearson to keep the peace on two sureties of £250 and Pearson valued his outraged honour at less than that sum.

During the same month as the duel fiasco, Robert relinquished the lease of the Midhope Moors, which had caused him so much trouble and anger during the last few years. He had hoped to get some compensation for all the improvements he had made there and the expensive frightening of poachers. When this was queried he withdrew his claim with characteristic generosity and proud lack of business sense:

> "Mr. Earnshaw [the agent] stated that you in consultation with him had expressed your surprise that I should have required any compensation for the expense to wch. I have been put by preserving the Moors. That being your feeling and mine not being guided by pecuniary considerations alone, I beg most distinctly to withdraw my claim for compensation."[56]

Robert grew sick as the hunting season of 1835 advanced. He moved uneasily from Round Green, where Sally was extraordinarily pregnant, to stay with his friend Fisher, the lawyer in Doncaster. Here there was more talk and more plans made for selling the coal which lay under his estates. Unwilling to admit that he was no longer, as Fisher told him, "Hale, strong and hearty, of all my Friends the most powerful in constitution,"[57] he moved fretfully from Doncaster to Leeds, where he consulted Dr. Hobson; later that evening he rode out to the Star and Garter at Kirstallbridge and from the hotel wrote again to Fisher about selling the coal.[58] That very day, though Robert had yet to hear of it, Sally gave birth to twins, James and John.[59]

He returned to Round Green weak and sick at heart. His home there was mortgaged and in perpetual chaos, the two small children now reinforced by these other two bastards at Sally's ample bosom, debts mounting, farms unmanaged; a family and countryside that by disapproval robbed him of all contact with his equals, driving him into the company of gamekeepers, seedy failures and public house bullies. Hard living, hard riding and above all hard drinking, hustled him to his doom uncommonly fast. News of his physical deterioration filtered through to Ouslethwaite, where William, his next brother, there had a consultation with their formidable mother[60]; he noted in his account book that this visit was "re Brother Robert". Three days later he made his way down to the bedlam at Round Green. What he found there must have frightened him: one can guess at the squalor and disarray, the dilapidated house and the squalling children. Sally perhaps wisely busying herself elsewhere and Robert, lying in his four-poster bed with chintz hangings and a white quilt,[61] unshaven and lack lustre.

---

[56] Robert Elmhirst to Hon. A. Bosville. Draft, 15 June 1835.
[57] Fredk. Fisher to Robert Elmhirst. 28 Nov. 1835.
[58] Robert Elmhirst to Fredk. Fisher. 27 Oct. 1835.
[59] Worsbrough Parish Register gives the date of their birth at the time of their baptisms.
[60] 12 Nov. 1835. William's Account Book.
[61] William started to have an exact inventory made at Round Green on 3 Dec. 1835.

William went back to Ouslethwaite, ambassador from some odd land cut off from civilisation for so long. He and his mother sent for Richard from Lincoln, who, with the double advantage of physicianship and brotherly affection, went on to visit Round Green. He must have persuaded Robert that everything was not entirely hopeless, got him dressed and aboard his gig for Leeds, where they changed to a coach more comfortable and not so stylish.[62] Robert sent a last note to Fisher: "I am much weaker," he wrote, "and intending leaving this for London on Thursday morning, if I can get my affairs squared sufficient to leave; pray my good fellow as I have not heard from you since I left you; let me see you without delay." Then, later and more urgently he scribbled:"I can't go without seeing you."[63]

When they reached London the two brothers went to stay at the Imperial Hotel by Covent Garden. So many things had to be done; not only were there physicians to be consulted, but it was soon obvious that there was a will to be made. Such essentials as these were always being postponed by the sick man, there were jolly London acquaintances who called on him, again and again the lawyers were asked to wait, to waste precious time checking legal phrases, to come back in the afternoon or next morning. Fisher's London agent, Charles Lever, had a tiresome job making foolproof Robert's apparently simple wishes. Letters between Lever in London and Fisher in Doncaster give a picture, both medical and legal, of what was happening:

"I received a note from Elmhirst this morning desiring me to call on him at the Imperial Hotel in Covent Garden at 11 this morning where I attended accordingly and found our friend in a more emaciated state than I expected, he said his Doctor informed him his disease was one of the heart and that he might go off *like a snuff* at any time, he does not appear to me as if he would live a week."

Robert told the lawyer that he wished to leave everything that he had in the world to his friend, Robert Atkinson, of Darfield, Esquire. Lever wrote it down in pencil on the back of a piece of paper. When he got back to his office in Bedford Row, his legal mind began to see the dangers of such a will: what would happen, for instance, if Atkinson died? Meanwhile, a note reached him from the sick man punctiliously ordering that since Robert Atkinson was a Gentleman and no Esquire, the draft will and its three copies should be so amended when they were brought for signature at noon next day.[64] By this will Robert had arranged with Fisher (doubtless the urgent call before he moved south) that his entire estate should be used to benefit Sally and the children; the Elmhirsts could fend for themselves.

Next day, said Lever: "I waited on Elmhirst at the appointed time, but, being then in bed and very weak and expecting someone else to call, he postponed the signing of his will to half-past three o'clock this afternoon."[65] Mean-

[62] 19 Nov. 1835. William E's Account Book.
[63] Robert Elmhirst to Fredk. Fisher. 17 Nov. 1835.
[64] Chas. Lever to Fredk. Fisher. 24 Nov. 1835.
[65] Same to same. 25 Nov. 1835.

while, Robert had been thinking of other ways of seeing that Sally and the children were provided for without the necessity of sacrificing the lands which his ancestors had tended for half a millennium. Three days later Lever was called again:

> "I received a note from Dr. Elmhirst this morning at breakfast desiring me to go on to the Imperial immediately as his brother wished to see me. I went and found our friend sitting up in his bedroom and looking much the same as before, he said the Doctors had told him he was very near his end, that his heart was now so much enlarged that it would soon not have room enough to play, he scarcely expected to live 24 hours longer . . . Elmhirst said that if his brother William would agree to secure £20,000 to Sally Baxter and her children, to your and Atkinson's satisfaction, he [William] should have the whole of his property, real and personal, instanter, to do what he liked with."[66]

And somewhat thus, with a great many legal complications and limitations, the will was finally made. Robert Atkinson was now named trustee and was to sell as much of the estate as would pay all debts and in addition raise £20,000. This £20,000 was to be shared equally between Sally and her four children, £4,000 apiece. What was left of the estate after the money had been raised was not to go to his good brother, but was to be held in trust for his nephews. In those three days history must have proved too much for the dying Robert, too strong even for the dislike he felt for his smug brother. Perhaps, too, he was influenced by the thought of his children, unmentioned in the first will, who now were named and acknowledged. One at least of their descendants is grateful.

Late on Saturday night the copies of the testament were taken round to the hotel for signature.

> "Elmhirst desired the will might be read slowly and distinctly over to him . . . When we came to the conclusion, where his brother William was described as residuary legatee, he said he hoped it was sufficiently clear that the £20,000 was to be paid first. I assured him that it was so and he was then satisfied only remarking that he was pretty sure his brother would elect to secure the £20,000, that if his health had permitted he would have planned the will better, but as the main purpose was answered he was satisfied, he shewed wonderful exertion in signing the will and duplicate, sheet by sheet, though in much weakness."[67]

On Monday, when Lever went round to Covent Garden with more suggestions and queries, he was startled to hear that early on Sunday morning the dying man had left with his brother for Yorkshire.

> "There was a gentleman there inquiring after him when I was (a stout, tall, good-looking man) who told me that although he doubted whether Elmhirst would reach Yorkshire alive, he was still not surprized at his making the effort knowing how resolute Elmhirst was in anything he had a mind to."[68]

---

[66] Chas. Lever to Fredk. Fisher. 28 Nov. 1835.
[67] Chas. Lever to Fredk. Fisher. 30 Nov. 1835.
[68] Same to same.

Robert, unused to suffering, surprised and angry, like a wounded animal, had fixed his steadfast gaze on Round Green; there he would go to earth and thither death must gallop after to dig him out if it could. Anything was better than to be killed so far afield, in a hired bedroom of a strange nightmare hotel filled with business men and city dwellers; where the air hung heavy with town noises and the market reek of long dead vegetables.

His gig they were forced to leave at Leeds, every jolt of more comfortable coaches increased his tiredness and his sickness. Back to squealing, shrill Round Green, where farmhands peered to see how the master looked. Somehow he got to bed, the bed he had made for himself, and there next day he died.

APPENDIX A

EARLIEST GENERATIONS OF PEDIGREE ACCORDING TO NORROY DUGDALE (1665)

(*Surtees Soc.*, Vol. XXXVI, p. 199)   (Coll. Arm. MS. C.40)

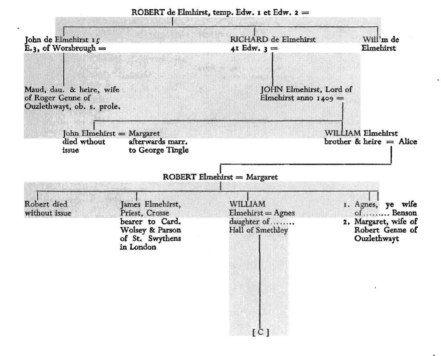

ROBERT de Elmhirst, temp. Edw. 1 et Edw. 2 =

John de Elmehirst 15
E.3, of Worsbrough =

RICHARD de Elmehirst
41 Edw. 3 =

Will'm de
Elmehirst

Maud, dau. & heire, wife
of Roger Genne of
Ouzlethwayt, ob. s. prole.

JOHN Elmehirst, Lord of
Elmehirst anno 1409 =

John Elmehirst = Margaret
died wthout   afterwards marr.
issue   to George Tingle

WILLIAM Elmehirst
brother & heire = Alice

ROBERT Elmehirst = Margaret

Robert died
without issue

James Elmehirst,
Priest, Crosse
bearer to Card.
Wolsey & Parson
of St. Swythens
in London

WILLIAM
Elmehirst = Agnes
daughter of ....
Hall of Smethley

1. Agnes, ye wife
   of .... Benson
2. Margaret, wife of
   Robert Genne of
   Ouzlethwayt

[C]

APPENDIX B

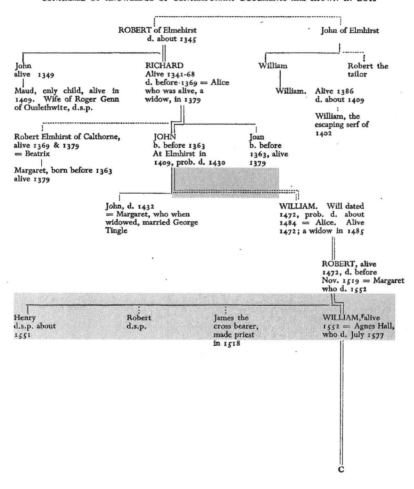

ROBERT of Elmehirst
d. about 1345

John of Elmhirst

John
alive 1349

Maud, only child, alive in
1409. Wife of Roger Genn
of Ouslethwite, d.s.p.

RICHARD
Alive 1341-68
d. before 1369 = Alice
who was alive, a
widow, in 1379

William

William. Alive 1386
d. about 1409

Robert the
tailor

William, the
escaping serf of
1402

Robert Elmhirst of Calthorne,
alive 1369 & 1379
= Beatrix

Margaret, born before 1363
alive 1379

JOHN
b. before 1363
At Elmhirst in
1409, prob. d. 1430

Joan
b. before
1363, alive
1379

John, d. 1432
= Margaret, who when
widowed, married George
Tingle

WILLIAM. Will dated
1472, prob. d. about
1484 = Alice. Alive
1472; a widow in 1485

ROBERT, alive
1472, d. before
Nov. 1519 = Margaret
who d. 1552

Henry
d.s.p. about
1551

Robert
d.s.p.

James the
cross bearer,
made priest
in 1518

WILLIAM, alive
1552 = Agnes Hall,
who d. July 1577

C

126

APPENDIX C

(Dates are in the modern style hereafter.)

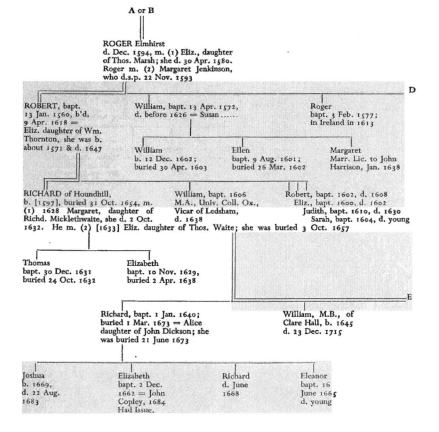

A or B

ROGER Elmhirst
d. Dec. 1594, m. (1) Eliz., daughter
of Thos. Marsh; she d. 30 Apr. 1580.
Roger m. (2) Margaret Jenkinson,
who d.s.p. 22 Nov. 1593

D

ROBERT, bapt.
13 Jan. 1560, b'd.
9 Apr. 1618 =
Eliz. daughter of Wm.
Thornton, she was b.
about 1571 & d. 1647

William, bapt. 13 Apr. 1572,
d. before 1626 = Susan ......

Roger
bapt. 3 Feb. 1577;
in Ireland in 1613

William
b. 12 Dec. 1602;
buried 30 Apr. 1603

Ellen
bapt. 9 Aug. 1601;
buried 26 Mar. 1602

Margaret
Marr. Lic. to John
Harrison, Jan. 1638

RICHARD of Houndhill,
b. [1597], buried 31 Oct. 1654, m.
(1) 1628 Margaret, daughter of
Richd. Micklethwaite, she d. 2 Oct.
1632. He m. (2) [1633] Eliz. daughter of Thos. Waite; she was buried 3 Oct. 1657

William, bapt. 1606
M.A., Univ. Coll. Ox.,
Vicar of Ledsham,
d. 1638

Robert, bapt. 1602, d. 1608
Eliz., bapt. 1600, d. 1602
Judith, bapt. 1610, d. 1630
Sarah, bapt. 1604, d. young

Thomas
bapt. 30 Dec. 1631
buried 24 Oct. 1632

Elizabeth
bapt. 10 Nov. 1629,
buried 2 Apr. 1638

E

Richard, bapt. 1 Jan. 1640;
buried 1 Mar. 1673 = Alice
daughter of John Dickson; she
was buried 21 June 1673

William, M.B., of
Clare Hall, b. 1645
d. 23 Dec. 1715

Joshua
b. 1669,
d. 22 Aug.
1683

Elizabeth
bapt. 2 Dec.
1662 = John
Copley, 1684
Had Issue.

Richard
d. June
1668

Eleanor
bapt. 16
June 1665
d. young

127

APPENDIX D

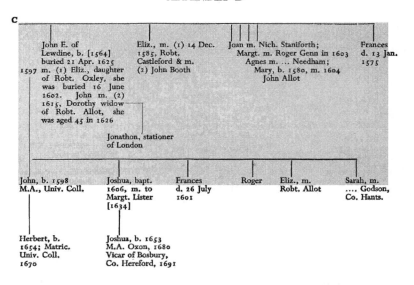

C

| John E. of Lewdine, b. [1564] buried 21 Apr. 1625 1597 m. (1) Eliz., daughter of Robt. Oxley, she was buried 16 June 1602. John m. (2) 1615, Dorothy widow of Robt. Allot, she was aged 45 in 1626 | Eliz., m. (1) 14 Dec. 1585, Robt. Castleford & m. (2) John Booth | Joan m. Nich. Staniforth; Margt. m. Roger Genn in 1603 Agnes m. ... Needham; Mary, b. 1580, m. 1604 John Allot | Frances d. 13 Jan. 1575 |

Jonathon, stationer of London

| John, b. 1598 M.A., Univ. Coll. | Joshua, bapt. 1606, m. to Margt. Lister [1634] | Frances d. 26 July 1601 | Roger | Eliz., m. Robt. Allot | Sarah, m. .... Godson, Co. Hants. |

| Herbert, b. 1654; Matric. Univ. Coll. 1670 | Joshua, b. 1653 M.A. Oxon, 1680 Vicar of Bosbury, Co. Hereford, 1691 |

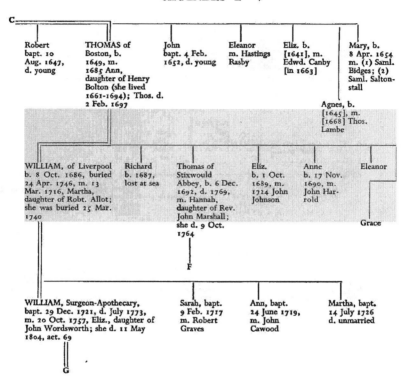

C

Robert
bapt. 10
Aug. 1647,
d. young

THOMAS of
Boston, b.
1649, m.
1685 Ann,
daughter of Henry
Bolton (she lived
1661-1694); Thos. d.
2 Feb. 1697

John
bapt. 4 Feb.
1652, d. young

Eleanor
m. Hastings
Rasby

Eliz. b.
[1641], m.
Edwd. Canby
[in 1663]

Mary, b.
8 Apr. 1654
m. (1) Saml.
Bidges; (2)
Saml. Salton-
stall

Agnes, b.
[1645], m.
[1668] Thos.
Lambe

WILLIAM, of Liverpool
b. 8 Oct. 1686, buried
24 Apr. 1746, m. 13
Mar. 1716, Martha,
daughter of Robt. Allot;
she was buried 25 Mar.
1740

Richard
b. 1687,
lost at sea

Thomas of
Stixwould
Abbey, b. 6 Dec.
1692, d. 1769,
m. Hannah,
daughter of Rev.
John Marshall;
she d. 9 Oct.
1764

Eliz.
b. 1 Oct.
1689, m.
1724 John
Johnson

Anne
b. 17 Nov.
1690, m.
John Har-
rold

Eleanor

Grace

F

WILLIAM, Surgeon-Apothecary,
bapt. 29 Dec. 1721, d. July 1773,
m. 20 Oct. 1757, Eliz., daughter of
John Wordsworth; she d. 11 May
1804, aet. 69

Sarah, bapt.
9 Feb. 1717
m. Robert
Graves

Ann, bapt.
24 June 1719,
m. John
Cawood

Martha, bapt.
14 July 1726
d. unmarried

G

APPENDIX F (to 1835)

E

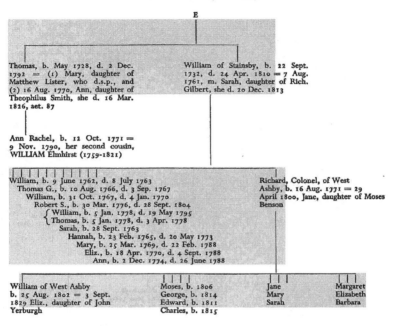

Thomas, b. May 1728, d. 2 Dec. 1792 = (1) Mary, daughter of Matthew Lister, who d.s.p., and (2) 16 Aug. 1770, Ann, daughter of Theophilus Smith, she d. 16 Mar. 1826, aet. 87

William of Stainsby, b. 22 Sept. 1732, d. 24 Apr. 1810 = 7 Aug. 1761, m. Sarah, daughter of Rich. Gilbert, she d. 20 Dec. 1813

Ann Rachel, b. 12 Oct. 1771 = 9 Nov. 1790, her second cousin, WILLIAM Elmhirst (1759-1821)

William, b. 9 June 1762, d. 8 July 1763
Thomas G., b. 10 Aug. 1766, d. 3 Sep. 1767
William, b. 31 Oct. 1767, d. 4 Jan. 1770
Robert S., b. 30 Mar. 1776, d. 28 Sept. 1804
{ William, b. 5 Jan. 1778, d. 19 May 1795
{ Thomas, b. 5 Jan. 1778, d. 3 Apr. 1778
Sarah, b. 28 Sept. 1763
Hannah, b. 23 Feb. 1765, d. 20 May 1773
Mary, b. 25 Mar. 1769, d. 22 Feb. 1788
Eliz., b. 18 Apr. 1770, d. 4 Sept. 1788
Ann, b. 2 Dec. 1774, d. 26 June 1788

Richard, Colonel, of West Ashby, b. 16 Aug. 1771 = 29 April 1800, Jane, daughter of Moses Benson

William of West Ashby b. 25 Aug. 1802 = 3 Sept. 1829 Eliz., daughter of John Yerburgh

Moses, b. 1806
George, b. 1814
Edward, b. 1811
Charles, b. 1815

Jane
Mary
Sarah

Margaret
Elizabeth
Barbara

APPENDIX G (to 1835)

E

WILLIAM, J.P. & D.L.,
bapt. 11 Apr. 1759,
d. 20 Sept. 1821, m. 9 Nov.
1790 his cousin Ann
Rachel (see Appendix F)

Thomas
bapt. 12 July
1763, buried 18
July 1763

Martha
buried 11 Jan.
1795, aet. 30

Elizabeth,
bapt. 18 Apr. 1761,
d. Sept. 1827 = 1784
Thos. Taylor [1737-1827]

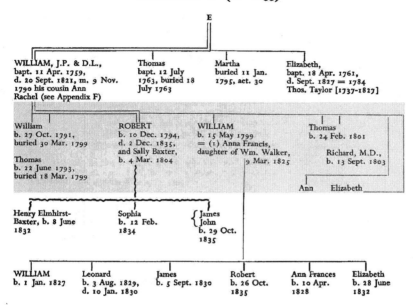

William
b. 27 Oct. 1791,
buried 30 Mar. 1799

Thomas
b. 22 June 1793,
buried 18 Mar. 1799

ROBERT
b. 10 Dec. 1794,
d. 2 Dec. 1835,
and Sally Baxter,
b. 4 Mar. 1804

WILLIAM
b. 15 May 1799
= (1) Anna Francis,
daughter of Wm. Walker,
9 Mar. 1825

Thomas
b. 24 Feb. 1801

Richard, M.D.,
b. 13 Sept. 1803

Ann   Elizabeth

Henry Elmhirst-
Baxter, b. 8 June
1832

Sophia
b. 12 Feb.
1834

{ James
{ John
b. 29 Oct.
1835

WILLIAM
b. 1 Jan. 1827

Leonard
b. 3 Aug. 1829,
d. 10 Jan. 1830

James
b. 5 Sept. 1830

Robert
b. 26 Oct.
1835

Ann Frances
b. 10 Apr.
1828

Elizabeth
b. 28 June
1832

APPENDIX H

THE ELMHIRST-CUTTS RELATIONSHIP

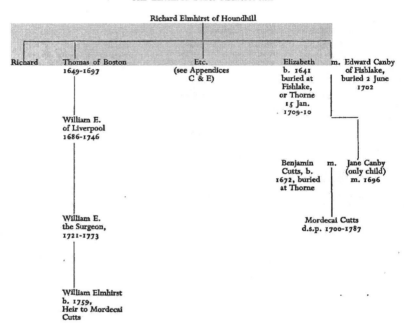

Richard Elmhirst of Houndhill

Richard

Thomas of Boston
1649-1697

Etc.
(see Appendices
C & E)

Elizabeth
b. 1641
buried at
Fishlake,
or Thorne
15 Jan.
1709-10

m. Edward Canby
of Fishlake,
buried 2 June
1702

William E.
of Liverpool
1686-1746

Benjamin
Cutts, b.
1672, buried
at Thorne

m. Jane Canby
(only child)
m. 1696

William E.
the Surgeon,
1721-1773

Mordecai Cutts
d.s.p. 1700-1787

William Elmhirst
b. 1759,
Heir to Mordecai
Cutts

APPENDIX K

The history of both the district and the family may be epitomised in the story of the few fields that form the property of Elmhirst, the peculiar inheritance.

The earliest settlement, prior to 1340, probably consisted of no more than the homestead, Laith Field and the Long Lands which still show the reason for their name. Here lived a bondman and his family in a small clearing among the forest elms at the northern extremity of the manor. The original homestead was almost certainly a long low building with the animals' quarters a lower continuation at one end, mutually warming in winter. Such a house of ancient form and too archaic to have a determinable date assigned to it still remains. Until recently this symbol of the family's origins was overshadowed by a pretentious early Victorian erection in a baronial style no less significant. This sham was pushed down in 1949 after less than a hundred years of existence, its fall hastened and made doubly desirable by land subsidences caused by the removal of the coal beneath. It was but justice that that which was born of coal should so perish by coal. The fields themselves, though mined and countermined, are more enduring.

WOOD ROYD, to the north of the homestead, would seem to be that same land that John of Elmhirst obtained in 1409 from Robert of Pilley, who may himself have reclaimed it from the forest. The name of Wood Royd means "wood clearing" and it was a new wood clearing to the north of Elmhirst that was transferred in that year.

WEST FIELD, to the north of Wood Royd, was probably part of the same transaction (two assarts or clearings are mentioned) by its name it could have been an accretion from some property lying to the east, either the Yews or Darley Cliff. Much more reasonable is the suggestion that the name West is a corruption of Waste. It was certainly part of Elmhirst prior to 1638 when it was copyhold together with the rest of the property. Far Field, to the north, adjoining the Barnsley borough district boundary, has been recently overbuilt. It was sold in 1917.

WARD GREEN is represented by two patches of land lying south of the homestead. These remain monuments to those particular vanished commons which, as elsewhere in the neighbourhood, were swallowed about the year 1820.

UPPER DAW CROFT AND NETHER DAW CROFT, together with what was once the related Daw Croft Wood, were part of Elmhirst before 1536; old countrymen living in the Armada year agreed that such had been the arrangement under "the late dissolved Nunnery of Nun Appleton". The word "croft" is of Saxon derivation and originally meant a small enclosed field adjacent to a house—land which was worked by the skill or "craft" of the householder himself.

OSMONDCROFT and the two other fields which form the southernmost projection of the property, were all added to Elmhirst in 1637 by prosperous Richard Elmhirst of Houndhill.

DAW CROFT ING, the middle of these three, has had the new Sheffield road driven like a stake through its heart.

DYKE ING, which seems to be the same as Ditching, was also bought by Richard from the Rockleys. This field, low-lying and once well-named, has been even more disturbed. Probably the least considered of the 1637 purchases, it became a tremendous family asset when the Dearne and Dove Canal stiffened the meandering river from its marshy bed in 1799. The lower part of Dyke Ing then became a canal wharf with the corresponding advantages, tactical and financial, that a wharf-holder, particularly if he was a coal-owner in addition, enjoyed throughout the Industrial Revolution. Now the marvel of 1799 is in its turn ignored, the water lies sluggish and ill-considered. Another corridor, the Victorian steam railway, was later laid down beside the canal in what was once the same damp field and this is at present (1951) being rejuvenated by electricity.

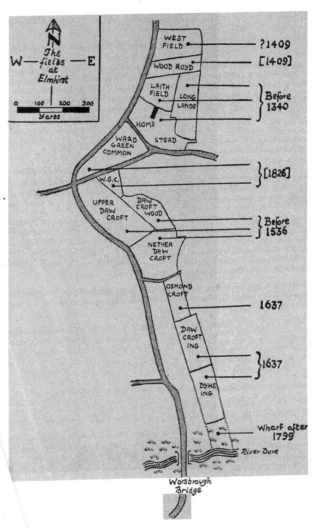

The fields at Elmhirst

W — E

0 100 200 300
Yards

WEST FIELD · · · · · · · ?1409
WOOD ROYD · · · · · · [1409]
LAITH FIELD
LONG LANDS · · · · · } Before 1340
HOME STEAD
WARD GREEN COMMON
W.G.C. · · · · · · · · } [1825]
UPPER DAW CROFT
DAW CROFT WOOD · · · · } Before 1536
NETHER DAW CROFT
OSMOND CROFT
· · · · · · · · · · · 1637
DAW CROFT ING · · · · } 1637
DYKE ING
· · · · · · · Wharf after 1799
River Dove
Worsbrough Bridge

INDEX

AINSWORTH, Fran., 36, 37
Aldwark, 43
Allen, 43, 87, 90
Allott, Dorothy, 36n
    Martha, 73
    Rich., 96
    Robt., 73
    Sarah, 73
    Thos., 13
Altringham, 48
Archdale, 75n
Ardsley, 60
Ashmore, Robt., 43
Askwith, Ald., 37
Atkinson, Robt., 122, 123
Aylmeherst, 16

BADSWORTH HUNT, 113, 119
Banker, Wm., 90
Bankhouse, 65
Bank Top, 29, 31
Barker, Thos., 67
Barnsley, 31, 42, 51, 62, 78
Barton, Wm., 55
Barugh, 48, 60
Bateman, Mary, 118
Baxter, Jas. and John, 121
    Sally, 112, 118, 121, 123
    Sophia, 119
Beale, 63
Beckett, Rich., 31
Beckwith, Wm., 53, 58
Beesley, Fran., 43
Beeston Park, 57
Belknap, Justice, 17
Benson, 23, 27
Bentley, Margt., 30
Bessy Bedlam, 113
Birks, 92, 106
Bland, Capt., 101
Bolton family, 66, 70
Bolton-on-Dearne, 17
Booth, Eliz., 34
    John, 34, 35, 40, 42, 59
Boston, 64, 66, 67, 68, 69, 71
Bradford, 106
Brigsley, 91
Broddesworth, Wm., 28

Brooke, Jopson, 43
Butler, Jane, 36n
Buxton, 95

CAMBRIDGE, Clare Hall, 62
Canby, Edwd., 62
Carpenter, 43
Carpet Weaver, 113
Carr, Jas., 98
Castleford, Eliz., 33, 34, 35
    Robt., 33, 34, 35
    Wm., 34
Catelyn, John, 16
Cawood, John, 29, 77
    Robt., 43
Cawthorne, 16
Chadwick, John, 43
    Saml., 83
Chapman, 43
Chatterton, Rich., 24n
Chorley, 75, 99, 118n
Christopher, John, 67
Clarissa, 111
Clayton, Baxter, 43
Clayton Hall, 74
Cliff, Robt., 14
Cockshutt, Jas., 102
College of Arms, 59, 62, 63, 64
Cooper, Rich., 85
Copley, Sir Godfrey, 65
    John, 65, 82
    Lionel, 57
    Robt., 71n
    Thos., 71n
Cotes, Hen., 6
Coulton, 56, 57, 60, 61
Cousins, Betty, 93
Cromwell, Oliver, 58
Crooks, Jas., 30
Culton, 43
Cutler family, 32, 73
Cutts, Mordecai, 90, 109

DANBY'S REGT., 50
Darfield, 13, 62
Darley Cliff, 34, 44, 133
Darton, 29, 60

Darton Club, 97
Davy, Thos., 16n
Dawcroft, 31, 43, 44, 133
Dearne River, 29
Dearne and Dove Canal, 94, 98, 102, 107, 133
Dickson, Alice, 62
Dixon, Jeremiah, 83
Doncaster, 13, 42, 51, 65, 99, 100, 103, 120
Dove, River, 10, 11n
Downing, Fran., 90
Drake, John, 91, 93
Dring, Thos., 58n
Dugdale, Sir Wm., 63, 64
Dyer, 73n, 90n
Dyke Ing, 48, 133
Dymoke, Sir Chas., 66

EARNSHAW, 95n, 116
Ecclesfield, 83
East Halton, 91
Edmunds, Fran., 80, 81, 82
    Hen., 65
    Thos., 51, 52, 57, 59
Ellis, 55, 78
Elmenhorst family, 49n
Elmhirst, the place, 5, 20, 29, 48, 49, 59,
    65, 72, 73, 74, 78n, 87, 133
Elmhirst, Agnes, 23, 25, 28, 29, 30
    Alice, 12, 14, 16, 21
    Ann, 68, 73
    Ann R., 91, 95, 96, 97, 106, 108
    Charles, 117n
    Eleanor, 61
    Eliz., 29, 30, 31, 33, 39, 45, 46,
        61, 64, 68, 83, 86, 88, 92, 101
    Ellen, 36n
    Frances, 30
    Henry, 23, 25, 27
    Herbert, 103n
    James, 23, 26, 117n
    Janet, 29
    Joan, 14, 16, 30
    John, 8, 9, 12, 14, 16, III, 20, 21,
        30, 33, 34, 35, 43, 61
    Joshua, 64, 65
    Judith, 33
    Margt., 19, 21, 23, 25, 30, 31, 33,
        36, 45, 46
    Martha, 73, 74, 77, 88, 96
    Mary, 30, 31
    Matilda, 12, 17

Rich., 8, II, 17, 33, IX, 61, 62, 68,
    72, 73, 75n, 101, 106, 109, 111,
    112, 113, 117, 119, 123
Robt., I, 17, 21, V, 29, VIII, 42,
    43, 62, 74, 85n, 96, XIV
Roger, 28, VII, 31n, 33, 34
Sarah, 33, 73, 75
Susan, 36
Thos., 46, X, 70, 72, 91, 94, 98
Wm., 8, 9, 10, 17, 18, IV, VI, 30,
    33, 35, 36n, 42, 44, 47, 48, 61,
    62, 64, 65, 68, 69, XI, XII, XIII,
    111
Elmhirst-Baxter, Hen., 81n, 118
Elmhurst, 49n
Enclosures, 102, 104, 109
Everett, Hugh, 38n
Everingham, Fran., 32, 33n
    Hen., 32

FAIRBURN, 55, 56, 60
Fairfax, Sir Thos., 52
    Sir Wm., 26
Fawkes, Fran., 102
Fells, Serjeant, 43
Fenton, Randle, 43
    Rich., 92n
Firth, Jonathan, 91
Fisher, Fredk., 119, 120, 121, 122
    John, 6, 7
    Peter, 10
    Wm., 11
Fishlake, 90
Flower, Mare, 78
Foxcroft, Eliz., 33
Frampton, 69
Fullers, 43
Furnivals Inn, 87

GAINSBROUGH, IDONEA, 14
Gelder, Thos., 82
Genn Farm and House, 47, 65, 72, 73, 74, 75,
    77, 78, 86, 87, 92, 98, 101
Genn, Margt., 27, 33
    Matilda, 17, 18n
    Roger, 17, 23, 33, 55
German, Hugh, 10n
Geye, 106
Glanvile, Surgeon, 84

Glewhouse, 47
Goldsmiths' Hall, 54, 55, 56, 57, 58
Greaves, Rich., 85
    Robt., 74, 77, 85
    Sarah, 75, 77
Greenland Co., 55

HAIGH, 100
Hall, Agnes, 25
    Fran., 73n
    Robt., 74n
    Sarah, 73n
    Thos., 74, 91, 93, 94
Hammersley, Thos., 75, 84
Hammerton, John, 89
Hangman Stone, 85
Hanson, Eliz., 35
    Gervase, 35, 36, 38 to 43
    Thos., 41
Hansworth Woodhouse, 34
Harman, 43
Harrison, Geo., 104
    John, 36
    Wm., 6
Hatfield, Eliz., 91
Haxby, 62
Hayes, John, 85, 86
Heaton, 96
Heeley, 47
Hemsworth, Eliz., 55
    Thos., 17
Higham, 48, 55
Hill, Fran., 78n
Hilly Close, 48
Hinchcliffe, Robt., 28n
Hirst, Geo., 89
Hodgson, John, 57
Hodroyd, 63
Houndhill, 27, 29, 31, 33, 37, 47, 48, 49, 51, 53, 58, 59, 60, 62, 64, 65, 71n
Howard of Effingham, Ld., 119
Howard, Mrs., 105
Hoyland Swain, 16, 60
Hoyle, Ald., 56
Hurst, John, 81

IMPERIAL HOTEL, London, 122
Iveson, 96

JENKINSON, Chas. and Margt., 30
Jewel, Mare, 78
Jowet Royd, 48

KAY, Sir John, 63
Kendal Green, 26n, 30, 31, 48
Kingswood, 31
Kirby Knowle, 48
Kitchinman, 43
Knowles, 104, 105, 110, 112

LAMB, John, 72
Ledsham, 48
Leeds, 65n, 118n, 124
Lees Hall, 65n
Lever, Chas., 122, 123
Lewdine, 36, 73
Limerick, 36
Lincoln's Inn, 104
Lister, Wm., 57, 63
Liverpool, 73
Longvillers, Clementia, 5, 8

MABB, 43
Macdonald, Ld., 115
Mainwaring, Sir Phil., 45
Marriott Family, 42
Marris, Rich., 47n
Marsden, John, 117n
Marsh, Eliz. and Thos., 29
Meaux Abbey, 13
Meager, Eliz., 70n
Medley, Nich., 40n
Merrell, John, 116
Micklethwaite, Eliz., 45, 48
    Rich., 45
    Wm., 31n
Middlebrook, Wm., 90n
Middleton, Ald., 43
Midhope Moor, 115 to 121
Miller, Wm., 11
Milnethorp, John, 11
Monk Bretton Priory, 13, 17, 25, 26, 29, 30, 33
Monkton, Capt., 63

NETHER HALL, 65
Nettleton, Dr., 75
Nevill, Sandford, 63
Newark, 72
Noble, John, 92
Northern Council, 45, 47, 51
Norton, Avery, 30
Nun Appleton Priory, 5, 8, 23, 25, 26, 43

OKE, Thos., 41
Osmondcroft, 48, 133
Oxclose, 48
Oxford, Univ. Coll., 44, 45
· Wadham Coll., 47
Oxley, Eliz., 34n
John, 79
Ouslethwaite, 33, 47, 65, 72, 75, 77, 78, 84,
86, 90, 91, 98, 105, 108, 111, 121

PARKER, Rich., 24n
Park House, 88
Parkin, 80, 89
Peace, Wm., 37
Pearson, John, 119, 121
Penistone, 26, 60
Pestor, Wm., 68
Pickering, Billy, 120
Pilkington, John, 24
Pilley, Robt., 20
Pontefract, 54, 58
Porter, Wm., 98, 99
Pulford, 57

RADCLIFFE, Sir Geo., 45, 50, 55, 56, 58, 59,
·60
Thos., 61
Randle, John, 43
Rasby, Eleanor, 70, 71, 72
Hastings, 70
Raylton, 57
Renishaw, 65
Rhodes, Sir Edwd., 58
Rich., 68
Wm., 80
Robinson, Fran., 37
Luke, 57
Rob Royd, 29, 77

Rock, Surgeon, 74, 85
Rockley Manor, 5 to 10, 14, 15
Rockley, Eliz., 17
Fran., 59
John, 6
Peter, 10
Robt., 17, 28, 52
Roscius, 101
Rotherham, 34, 51
Rothwell, 60
Round Green, 100, 110 to 113, 118, 121 to
123

ST. JOHN'S CHURCH, London, 55
St. Peter's Church, London, 36n
St. Swithin's Church, London, 23, 24
Saltonstall, Rich., 71n
Sandal, 54
Sawyer, Jas., 30
Louis, 31n
Schofield, 94, 96
Seyll family, 23, 27n
Shay, Josh., 82, 84
Sheffield, 51, 98, 103, 116
Sheffield, Sir Robt., 114
Sherburne, Rich., 50
Shirt, Geo., 87n
Silkstone, 30, 31, 73, 87n
Simonson, Rich., 10n
Sitwell, Geo., 65
Sitwell, 96
Skegness, 106
Slade Hooton, 30
Smith, Theophilus, 91
Smithley, 25
South Ottrington, 48, 54
Sporting Magazine, 114
Stainbrough, 5, 31, 32
Staincross, 30, 63, 100
Stanhope, Spencer, 87n, 102
Star Inn, Barnsley, 63
Stewart, Hen., 56, 57
Stixwould, 66, 91, 93
Stone, Walt., 24n
Stonehall, 69
Stonyhurst, 50
Swaith, 26, 45, 73n, 93, 98
Swinnow Park, 109
Sykehouse, 90
Sykes, Jas., 89
Sir Tatton, 115
Syntax, Dr., 111

TANTIVY, 101n
Tattershall, John, 78
Taylor, Eliz., 88, 109, 113
    Robt., 16n
      Thos., 88, 89
Tempest family, 33
Thorne, 62, 90, 109
Thornton, Eliz. and Wm., 33
Thorpe, Saml., 96
Thurgoland, 102
Tingle, Geo., 21
Turf Tavern, 120
Turton, John, 65, 72n

USSELBY HOUSE, 106, 108, 114
Uvedale, Sir Thos., 50

VIRGINIA, 73

WAGSTAFFE, Dr., 80
Waite, Eliz. and John, 47
Walker, Anna, 109
    Hen. and Nich., 43
    Obadiah, 44, 83
    Wm., 31n, 85
Watson, Josh., 90n
Wells, Thos., 84
Went, John, 14
Wentworth Woodhouse, 44, 47
Wentworth, Sir Geo., 57, 59n
        Sir Thos., 44, 48 to 51, 56, 59,
        60
        E. of Strafford, 74n, 92
West, Jonathan, 89

Wheats, 103, 115
Wheledale, 60
White Bear Inn, 84
Whitley, 85
Wigfall, Rich., 7
Winder, Benj., 109n
Wolsey, Thos., 23
Wombwell, 13
Womersley, 72
Wood, Geo., 87
    Rich., 43
Woodhead, John, 72n
Woodhouse, John, 6
    Isabel, 7
Woods, John, 68
Wooley, Rich. and Wm., 28
Wordsworth, Eliz., 83, 86
    John, 62n, 83
Worlaby, 91
Worsbrough Church, 12, 28n, 30, 46, 65, 72,
      73, 75, 78, 80, 83, 96
    Manor and Court, 8, 9, 20, 34,
      40, 41, 42, 47, 53, 57, 65, 87,
      92, 104
    School, 28, 83
    Workhouse, 74n, 77, 82
Worsbroughdale, 26, 31, 48, 49, 52, 55, 62,
    74
Wortley, Sir Fran., 43, 52
Wright, John, 43
Wroot, 90
Wulthwaite, John, 6

YORK, 40, 45, 50 to 53, 58, 60, 61, 92
    Courant, 86
    St. Helen's Ch., 45, 46, 60, 61, 72
    St. Mary's Tower, 49, 53
    Trinity Church, 60

No. 132
of
200 printed.
E.

Printed by
KITCHEN & BARRATT, LTD.,
PARK ROYAL ROAD,
LONDON, N.W.10.